HOME SCHOOL HELL

With Saint Corona Up to Bat

A Widowed Father's 70 Days in E-Learning Captivity

Home School Hell

With Saint Corona Up to Bat

By Dave Heilmann

Print: 978-1-944027-79-7

EBook: 978-1-944027-80-3

For Natalie, Joey, Mikey, Brooke

and Erica

TABLE OF CONTENTS

A LETTER
MARCH 20, 2020

Dear Erica,

You wouldn't believe what is happening on Earth, honey. There is this virus that has hit the entire world. I know that sounds crazy, but it's real. They think it originated from a bat in China in 2019. It didn't bite anyone. The virus somehow jumps from the bat to humans, which is a little creepy. They call it coronavirus disease or COVID-19.

It started spreading in the United States in January, and by mid-March, schools were closing. First, it was only for two weeks to slow the spread of infection. But things just kept getting worse. Erica, a lot of people are dying. The people it's hitting the hardest are the seniors and those who have compromised immune systems, like people with cancer, diabetes, and lung conditions.

You would have been high-risk, sweetheart. How I wish I had the chance to hold you and protect you from it. The kids are doing okay, and your mom and dad are being careful, especially with your dad's emphysema. I've kept it to myself, but the thought of orphaning our children is terrifying.

People of all ages are dying. It usually starts with a cough and fever and, in the bad cases, can cause pneumonia, blood clotting, and organ failure. There hasn't been anything like this since the Spanish flu in 1918.

Stores have been closing and states across the country, including Illinois, have issued emergency orders that people have to stay at home, "shelter-in-place," except for those needing or working in essential businesses. Churches are closed. Grocery stores and gas stations are open, but restaurants are restricted to drive-through or curbside pickup.

I know what you're thinking—it's Natalie's senior year. She is supposed to have prom, graduation, and all the fun that comes with the last few months of high school. It's not looking good. Right now, they are still trying to give them a prom and graduation—in July.

You always told your mom that "if anything happens, you have to help Dave." And she has been, incredibly, three days a week. That has stopped because we can't take the risk, and she feels terrible about it. I do too because I've never seen so much laundry. Dear God, can they wear anything twice without it going in the laundry?

There's a new phrase: "social distancing." It means you have to stay at least six feet from other people because the virus is so contagious. The experts believe that if you're at least six feet away, the respiratory droplets from a cough or sneeze aren't likely to be inhaled. It's not like we're used to where you simply stay away from people who are sick. People are contagious before they feel any symptoms. Some people get it and never feel any symptoms.

If you get the disease and are breathing okay, they tell you to stay at home because the hospitals are filling up. When you stay at home with the disease, you also have to "quarantine" for fourteen days, away from others in your home. People are staying in their bedrooms, in basements. Surreal.

Everywhere you look people are wearing masks. Can you believe it? Masks. And they're running out of these. Everyone is hoarding masks, toilet paper, paper towels, cleaning supplies, and hand sanitizer. Even Amazon is sold out.

We're glued to the news, listening for "the COVID numbers," daily conferences on how many infections, how many deaths, and how to stay safe.

It is like no time before it in our lives.

And it witnessed the birth of compulsory remote learning, or learning from home, for every student in America. An Enlightenment, of sorts. For the sake of preserving history for our children, I took notes.

It was something to write home about.

THE VIRUS HITS HOME

On Friday, March 20, 2020, the State of Illinois has 585 confirmed cases of the COVID-19 virus, with five deaths.

The order that many feared is handed down.

Illinois residents will be ordered to "shelter-in-place" beginning March 21, 2020 at 5:00 p.m. and ending April 7, 2020.

Four children in lockdown at the end of a school year. Natalie, the high school senior; Joey, the high school freshman; Mikey, the seventh-grader and our baby Brooke, third grade. We lost the light of our lives, their mom and my bride Erica, in September 2018.

We can do this.

We aren't exactly sure what shelter-in-place means because it's never happened before. All we're told is that back in 1918 during the Spanish flu, St. Louis had a shelter-in-place and Philadelphia didn't. Philly had a parade instead and then everyone died, making it the worst parade ever.

But we have our orders, and we'll try and figure them out. I read my Chicago Tribune daily, and the March 20 article tries to offer some insight to parents as to what is coming:

"The order allows liquor stores and recreational cannabis dispensaries to remain open for business should the second week of impromptu homeschooling create an essential need."

Should the second week of impromptu homeschooling create an essential need?

It can't be that hard. Who doesn't love being with their children every second? Every second.

SATURDAY, MARCH 21: DAY 1

5:00 p.m.

The shelter-in-place begins.

I don't know why they have to come up with cute phrases like that. It's not a tornado. Is "stay at home" confusing to people?

We live in a south suburb of Chicago, an area commonly known as "the south side." When people ask where you're from, you say the name of the Catholic parish. "Where'd you grow up?" "St. John Fisher."

We're taught around here that no matter what problem you have, there's a patron saint for it. They cover anything. Saint Anthony—patron saint of things that can't be found. Saint Drogo—patron saint of ugly people. Great assignment for all of eternity.

Who upstairs is in charge of the pandemic? That's the first question for our neighborhood. What we are hearing, if you can believe this, is…Saint Corona. Not a joke. That's what was circulating. Truth is that her assignment for 1500 years prior to the virus was being the patron saint of treasure hunters. Not sure why that wasn't under Anthony's jurisdiction.

But regardless, look up Saint Corona on Wikipedia, the source of all truth, and the first paragraph now says, "Corona is venerated in connection with treasure hunting and the COVID-19 pandemic." Let's make sure we are clear about this. She is not going to have anything to do with other pandemics or world plagues. It's only COVID-19, a niche practice.

Natalie attends Mother McAuley, an all-girls Catholic high school. Joey is at Brother Rice, the all-male Catholic high school. In the true Catholic tradition of temptation, these schools are located five hundred yards from each other. Rumor has it that there is an underground tunnel connecting the schools, but no Rice guy will venture through for fear that it's being guarded by the Sisters of Mercy.

The Catholic schools aren't high-tech. That means we won't be having "virtual school" every day with interactive classrooms. For the most part, the students will be given assignments to complete by the end of the day. I'll worry about that on Monday when it starts.

Tonight I told the kids that at least I stocked up on a few things from Sam's Club last week. We won't need cups because I bought 500 of them. That should mean a few less dishes.

"Dad, are you talking about that box in the garage?" Joe asks.

"Yeah. Big box on a table," I tell him.

"You bought 500 lids. There are no cups in that box. It's just a box of lids."

That's ridiculous. They don't sell lids separately from cups. Who the hell would buy 500 lids?

I would.

It's Saturday night. Stay up, watch a movie, have popcorn, and use every glass in the house.

MARCH 22: DAY 2

The Governor of Illinois is JB Pritzker. He has the roundest head. Somewhat of a cross between former Governor Blagojevich and Buddy Hackett.

The governor announces another 296 cases, bringing the state total to 1,049, with nine deaths. Natalie is watching the governor's announcement, including his explanation for why we need to stay home.

"Dad, the Pritzkers own the Hyatt Hotels, don't they?"

"Yes, they do, honey."

"Well then they have about 900 homes, so it's easy for him to say stay home."

Logical. The kids aren't happy. "It's like being grounded without doing anything wrong," Joey says.

He's right. We're all pretty much grounded, the worst punishment. I hated it growing up. My mom grounded me in seventh grade from going to a roller-skating party. I had a crush on a girl who I knew would be there. I begged my mom to let me go.

"No. You're in. Maybe you'll think about that the next time."

I'll think about it for forty-three years is what I'll do. That girl ended up marrying a rich guy with fantastic hair who will probably never get the virus.

Every parent knows we have to follow the rules. Every parent wants their children to keep up with schoolwork during this stay-at-home period, because their education is so important. Unfortunately, I really don't care about any of that right now because I have a different problem.

We're supposed to go on a trip April 12th to see crazy Aunt Di Di and Uncle Kurdles. Di is my sister, a second mom to my children and every niece and nephew. She's the one my kids and their cousins love to be with because she's a box of holy shit fun.

So we cancel the flight and reschedule, right? Well, this happened to be the first time, the first time in my life, I have ever purchased first class airfare. I can still hear the agent's voice, "You understand that these first-class tickets are not refundable?" "Yes." Years of flying history where I always walked past those people in the large seats with the Lululemon outfits and good skin, on my way to the back of the plane. Not this trip. We are going first class. That was to be the big Easter morning surprise.

Worldwide pandemic closes the Earth. Surprise!

6:00 p.m.

Here come the robocalls. Every phone in the house rings. Recorded messages from the principals of the schools. I pay for a landline and hate everyone who calls on it.

8:00 p.m.

Wait, there is an upside to no school. I don't have to make lunches. I hate making lunches.

Tomorrow begins an education that I will never forget.

MARCH 23: DAY 3

The First Monday

I stay at home. The kids are all home. They have to learn in the home. I know we're calling it remote, distance or e-learning, but it feels a lot like homeschooling. I hear that phrase and picture parents standing in a barn giving lessons before the fields are plowed.

Have you ever had people tell you that they homeschool their kids? I have. I never knew what to say. My first thought was, "Who has the problem, you or the kid?" I know that's wrong.

Now I have to do it. It's not how I was trained.

In grammar school I was taught by nuns. There was one named Sister Stella, who had hundreds of little teeth in a pale, bloodless face. A classmate named Peter mentioned that he heard about a kid who was homeschooled. She rolled her eyes and told us that the boy was a nogoodnik and likely would end up in prison. After that, it was on to southern hell.

My youngest two go to this same school that I attended. It's called Saint Linus. No one's ever heard of that saint but he was the second pope after Peter. It's like singing right after Lady Gaga.

Here's the problem. The principal now is the same girl who sat at the desk in front of me every year when we were in school. Her name is Margaret. She would always snicker that she was smarter than me. Being a polite child, I would simply respond that I respectfully disagreed with her assessment. Or words to that effect. Anyhow, with this little remote learning gig, she's going to be checking every assignment of my kids. One question wrong and it'll be, "Did your father help you with this? Tell your father I knew I was smarter than him." That then becomes a mandatory subject of parent-teacher conferences for five years.

I can't live with that.

3:30 p.m.

Up to this point, the day has been uneventful.

"Dad?" Brooke calls.

"Yes?"

"I don't understand this," she says.

"What subject?" I ask from the other room.

"English. We have to diagram sentences."

Oh, dear God. All I remember is getting yelled at for not knowing how to do this. Can't we just say the words? Why do we have to put them on slanted lines? This was the assigned question:

> Think about your birthday. Write and diagram four sentences with prepositional phrases, two with direct objects, and two with compound predicates. And then diagram each sentence.

Well, for starters, you've ruined my birthday.

Let's read the lesson:

> To diagram a direct object, first write the subject and the verb in the horizontal line of the diagram. Write the

direct object on the horizontal line to the right of the verb.

Draw a vertical line between the verb and the direct object. This line touches the horizontal line but does not cut through it. A preposition is then written on a slanting line. The object of a preposition is written on a horizontal line connected to the slanting line with the preposition. The parts of a compound direct object are written on separate parallel lines after the verb and the coordinating conjunction is written on a vertical dashed line between the two parts.

Dad's answer: Brooke has a low-grade fever and, given the virus concerns, will not be able to do today's assignment.

For the record, I didn't give up. I went to the encyclopedia Google, where I take all of life's problems, and looked up the benefits of diagramming sentences. One enthusiastic supporter of diagram torture wrote:

"There is no easier way to teach the difference between direct objects and prepositional phrases. They just pop off the page!! AND, it's really fun for the logically inclined. I love it for untangling complicated seventeenth-century prose and understanding antecedents in biblical passages."

That does sound like fun. Instead of Silly String at the next birthday we'll have the kids untangle some prose.

That's our learning for today.

MARCH 24: DAY 4

There is this website called PearsonRealize.com. It's one of the places where the online educational materials are accessed. There are lessons, questions, and tests for students at every level. I'm not sure who decides the content for this website, but it is in "alignment with state standards."

Today's work for the high school freshman world history class had this question on Pearson Realize:

ASSESSMENT

How were the Moche able to farm along the arid coast of Peru in 100 A.D.?

First thought, café mocha. Thought two, how do I pronounce it? It's *Moh Chay*, which actually sounds more French than Spanish. I looked up Moche in French to see the translation to English. It means ugly. You'd think someone would have told them this.

I honestly have no idea how the Moche were able to farm in Peru or whether their vegetables were any good. This officially falls under the Doctrine of Who Cares, but who am I to criticize? The education standards tell us that the most important purpose for social sciences is for students to emerge with knowledge, skills, attitudes, and behaviors necessary to be informed and effective citizens.

I know my kids have the attitudes, so we're partially there. I do want them to be informed and effective citizens; would hate to have them go through life knowing nothing about how the Moche were able to farm. It would be an empty existence.

Answer: They lived in the deserts below the Andes Mountains in northern Peru. (Think Amazon Rainforest and Machu Picchu and you're in the right area.) Anyhow, these folks built extensive irrigation canals down from the Andes that helped them grow crops.

My head is full from all I've learned today, but I still have to work —from home. I feel guilty. I don't want to be the dad we always hear about, the one who spent all his time at work and never paid any attention to his children. That comes out in the first three minutes of the eulogy.

Give them your time, right? Give your children your time. They want it more than any other gift, than any vacation. This, I see but fail to recognize often enough.

4:00 p.m.

Joe is awake and has a vocabulary-builder assignment.

> Obstreperous: Noisy and hard to control. Use in a sentence.

The obstreperous children forced the father to drink in the morning.

I have also learned by this second day of e-school that their work is completed in a much shorter period of time than a typical school day. That means more time on their hands. Natalie decides that we need to find a game we can play that will take up a lot of time.

Monopoly. Great game. Takes forever.

We start at 8:15. The entire family is sitting around a table playing a board game, like it was 1957. Warm family picture, isn't it? Took eleven minutes for Joe to call his little brother a butthole for buying B&O Railroad, because Joe owned one of the railroads.

I'm watching my children buy every property they land on, except the purple junk. Their debt gets a bit heavy as Dad starts putting houses on the light blues and oranges.

"This is a good lesson for you," I tell them. "If you spend too much and are always in debt, you'll never get ahead."

"Boring, Dad," I'm told by the nine-year-old. She's right. Enough learning for Tuesday.

MARCH 25: DAY 5

There are now 65,000 COVID-19 cases in the United States and nearly one thousand deaths. We're all getting to know Dr. Anthony Fauci, the immunologist and Director of the National Institute of Allergy and Infectious Diseases (NIAID) since 1984. Any agency director who can survive six presidential administrations must be excellent.

Airlines have announced massive flight cancellations, except for mine. It might be the only one that's still on time.

In local news, a north side gas station owner is being investigated for selling single-ply toilet paper for five dollars per roll. There's a person who deserves years of car diarrhea.

But I have a bigger problem. I just read the assignment posted by the third-grade teacher for this morning. Common Core math. Cue the horror film music.

I want to know who came up with this. I would like a name. Instead of studying the canals built by these fine folks in the Andes in 100 AD, every parent for the rest of eternity needs to know the name of the person who decided that we need to do charts, arrays, pies, rows, columns, tables, and bar diagrams to figure out that 6 x 8 = 48.

Do you know why 6 x 8 is 48? Because it is. It always will be. That's the cool thing about math. There's this eerie certainty to it. Mrs. Dooley taught us in third-grade "to memorize your multiplication tables." Then she went and had a cigarette.

When I turn to the page with the assignment for today, it's titled "Common Core Performance Assessment." What happened to calling it a "problem?" Are there parents who actually ask their kids, "Have you completed your Common Core performance assessment today? "Yes, Father. Winston and I are both done. Mum said you'd take us for a yacht ride after we floss."

Today's problem:

Common Core Performance Assessment

Tony's Summer Jobs

Walking Dogs	$8/hour
Mowing Lawns	$10/hour
Running Errands	$3/hour

The table above shows how much Tony earns per hour for his summer jobs. One day Tony spends three hours running errands. He wants to use the money to buy two banners, which cost $9 each.

Okay, Tony, three hours at $3 each. Looks like you have nine bucks. You can buy one banner. Keep working, buddy. Are we done?

No. Not even close. Common Core has this tortured methodology where you have to start at the base of your brain and drag it up to the cerebral cortex.

1. Use Appropriate Tools: Choose a tool to represent the problem and explain why you chose that tool.

Tools? Where did tools come into play? Am I missing something? We're talking about Tony, a fourteen-year-old kid without a work permit doing odd jobs, and he wants to buy banners. All you need are the numbers here, not tools.

2. Make Sense and Persevere: What do you need to find out before you can solve the problem?

Need to know the name of the person who started Common Core math. Everything else we have. And "make sense and persevere" is borderline smarmy.

3. Does Tony have enough money? Use what you know to solve the problem.

Sure. I know that 3 x 3 = 9 and that Tony needs to cut my lawn.

1:30 p.m.

I never realized until we were all home all day how many little beeps and buzzers and jingles go off.

The microwave beeps when you touch the time, beeps when it's done, and, if you don't get your food out, continues beeping every ten seconds. Dryer has the game show "wrong answer" buzzer. Washing machine plays a jingle when the cycle ends. I don't understand why that jingle was added by manufacturers. Is it a belief that people would forget it ever happened and not return?

The refrigerator starts beeping if you don't close the door five seconds after opening it. Sometimes I'm not done that fast. Beeeeeeeeeeeeeeeeeeeeeeeep, Beeeeeeeeeeeeeeeeeep.

Now add five phones, a few iPads, some Chromebooks, the video games, and, of course, Amazon Prime and it's like sitting in the monitored ICU bed.

8:30 p.m.

We are back at the Monopoly game. Joey's still the banker handing out the money. Mikey is in charge of handing over hotels and houses, which I am covering my properties with.

Mikey is downing two sixteen-ounce homemade frappuccinos, the perfect evening drink for children.

I know this is precious time with them. Every parent feels like we just brought the baby home from the hospital and you blink and they're off to college.

We ask the same question our parents did: Where does the time go? Maybe it doesn't "go" anywhere. Maybe it comes when it isn't on the schedule like the perfectly planned vacation. Maybe it comes in the middle of the worst pandemic of a lifetime.

That's what I learned today.

MARCH 26: DAY 6

They don't get up in the morning. My plan was to have some structure so they got up each morning, ate, and started their schoolwork. This would leave plenty of free time for the video games, texts, and whatever else they wanted.

Sure, Dad.

It's hard to describe the look my oldest gives me when I ask her to get up in the morning. There's this swivel of her head on her neck, like Linda Blair in *The Exorcist*, and I get a "Who are you? I wish you were on fire!" stare.

As for the high school son, he joined the thousands playing Xbox until whatever hour. When I tell him to get up, he responds, "Why? The homework is due at midnight and there's nothing else to do." I hate when they use logic.

The seventh-grade literature assignment for Mikey today is reading comprehension for a document called 'Strange Medicine.'

I figure that reading about any kind of medicine should be a positive during a health epidemic. This was the worksheet:

Strange Medicine

Science and medicine have come a long way over the past years. Doctors understand a lot about how the body works, but they weren't always on the right track. Here are some interesting medical practices.

Leeching: Doctors first placed leeches on patients in order to draw out the bad spirits, or "humors," in a person. Today leeches can be helpful at removing blood from wounds.

Trepanation: Patients have a hole drilled, scraped, or hammered into their skull, allowing brain tissue to be permanently exposed. It was used 10,000 years ago and our chart says that this doesn't really work today.

Maggots: Maggots are poured into a wound so they can eat diseased and rotting tissue and even today "it is effective in cleaning wounds."

My spine is curling. I don't ever recall reading in my literature classes about the multiple ways a hole can be bored into your head or the upside to maggot therapy.

A few hours later Mikey calls me from the bathroom. I walked to the door and asked him if he was okay.

"No, I'm throwing up and pooping at the same time."

"Was it the literature assignment?" I ask.

I go and grab a bucket. I would normally bring it in the bathroom and help him, like any parent.

So many thoughts go through my head in the seconds I am bringing back the bucket. Does he have the virus? I can't get too close because one doctor said that in a small room the virus can aerosolize and infect rapidly. Fauci says at least six feet. I'm hearing about more and more people my age dying.

In an act of compassion, I opened the door and kicked the bucket over to him. Then when he was done, I asked my daughter to clean up the mess because she had a better chance of living through the infection.

I'm hoping that this is just a random flu, but who's thinking that these days? Off to Google to check for all symptoms of COVID-19.

It lists the following:

- Chills
- Shortness of breath
- Headache
- Sore throat
- Loss of taste or smell
- Muscle pain.

Great. He has none of those.

Next paragraph: There it is. "Some people may develop gastrointestinal symptoms such as diarrhea and vomiting."

Next stop, WebMD.

Look at this. A study by Dr. Wenbin Li, from the Department of Pediatrics at Tongji Hospital in Wuhan, China, says that children suffering from digestive tract symptoms should be suspected of having this virus. It may be the first manifestation of the disease.

It's in the house. I know it's in my house.

Mikey goes up to bed and has to be quarantined.

Natalie doesn't think he has it. "How could Mikey get it? He hasn't been out of the house. He's been the best one of all of us."

That's true. He hasn't been in contact with anyone outside of our house for several days.

The hell with him for a second. Two nights ago, I kissed him good night on the forehead. Do I have the virus now? My brain is trying to analyze whether my lips in contact with open pores in the forehead could contaminate. The kids should have me put away.

A few hours later, early in the evening, Mikey wakes up and is hungry. I set the plate down outside his door. As I walk away, my heart sinks. This isn't what moms and dads do. We don't walk away from our children when they're sick. We walk to them and hold them. We stay right at their side because that's where we belong. That's been taken away.

It makes me think about all those with a family member in a nursing home, many of whom are dying, and how their children will be unable to be with them at that moment. That's supposed to be the moment the child returns the love to his mom or dad for every day they held his hand when he was sick. Taken away.

I can't wait to hug my son. It will be a long one. Unless he coughs.

MARCH 27: DAY 7

Landline rings. "Hi, this is Melvin Rasbauer and I'm calling because this is your last chance to buy an extended warranty for your vehicle."

That was a real name. Melvin Rasbauer. My dad told me to never buy extended warranties from anyone named Melvin so I hung up.

Shouldn't these callers be sheltering at home? I'm very concerned about their health. They could become one of those clusters. For their safety, all the solicitors who call landlines should remain at home for six to eight years until the virus clears.

World history today. Pearson Realize. Ancient Middle East and Egypt 3200 B.C. – 500 B.C.

It looks like we're covering 2700 years in eleven pages. How would that make those people feel? That's not even one word per year.

Section 1: A Civilization Emerges in Sumer

The very first thing on this page is a picture of a man who is bent over, picking a plant in a garden. The plant is by a snake. Behind him is a man who has a normal torso, but his head is a horse. Did I miss that class when we talked about people in 3200 B.C. who had horseheads?

The caption under this picture reads:

> Gilgamesh, King of Uruk, sought eternal life and obtained the plant of youth. However, a snake ate it, which, according to legend, is why people do not live forever.

And now, because of this, very few children today are named Gilgamesh.

The assignment for today includes this question:

> How did the Hittites contribute to the cultural diffusion of early Mesopotamian culture and ideas, and what was one of the important technological advancements?

I'm going with the steam engine or the reaper. Those were always my fallbacks.

1:30 p.m.

I'm trying to get Mikey some food in his prison and the landline rings again. I almost didn't answer it figuring it was another sales call, but when it rings sixty-four times, I know it's my mother-in-law, Leona.

Great woman. Hates birds. Runs from them. She had one of those bouffant hair-dos in the '50s, and a bird flew into her hair and got stuck. Was pecking her head. Terrified ever since.

She's a spicy Italian and has been a hairdresser in one of Chicago's classic southside neighborhoods by Midway Airport for more than fifty years.

"Dorothy called me," Leona says. "You remember her. She's the one who can only see out of one eye because of the stroke."

They all get identified by medical status and condition.

"She wants me to come over to her house and cut her hair. I thought, what the shit, I'm not going over there."

Only my Italian friends and relatives use that phrase "what the shit." Never made sense to me but I'm accustomed to it.

"I told her I'm not going over to your house, Dorothy, not with this disease going around," she continues. "Where are you going anyway? The only place you go is to church and that's closed. She's all twisted. She's twisted." Twisted is the word Leona uses to describe when someone is upset without good reason.

"Anyway, I cracked a tooth. I don't know when I'll be able to see a dentist," she says. "How are the kids? How's my Mikey?"

"So far he's been okay today," I tell her. "He hasn't really been exposed to anyone with the virus so maybe it was a bug."

"Okay, well, I just wanted to check in. And that's it. That's it."

Leona ends most every call with the same phrase: *And that's it. That's it.* This means she doesn't have anything else to report. I tease, but she is a godsend to our lives.

3:00 p.m.

A $2 trillion economic stimulus bill became law today. It is the largest stimulus package in American history.

4:30 p.m.

Total coronavirus cases in Illinois currently stand at 488. Thirty-four people have died. I find myself checking the media reports more than I ever have.

I hope Mikey is okay.

MARCH 28: DAY 8

It's Saturday. Made it through the first week of e-learning.

My local grocery store is called Mariano's. I used to go there about 5-6 times a week and my family abused me for this. "Why can't you make a list and do it all at once?" they'd ask.

Because I wanted to stay under fifteen items and get through the express lane, that's why. I felt that those who went through that lane with more than fifteen items should be incarcerated. But it doesn't matter now because they put in self-serve checkouts that talk to you.

Today I'm there getting ice cream because I need two boxes of those mini-Dove bars. I rationalize the cost because it's a pandemic and you take whatever steps necessary to survive.

I see a neighbor from down the block. Good guy.

He says to me, "Hey neighbor, you holding up okay?"

"I am. How about you?"

"We're doing okay," he says. "I can't believe they're out of toilet paper everywhere." And then he paused, almost dramatically, and says, "We're down to, like, six rolls. I may have to borrow some from you."

He has this gleam in his eye. Like he knows something.

Does he know I have two Charmin 24 = 96 Ultra Strongs sitting in the garage? They're four times stronger when wet versus the leading bargain brand. His kids play with my kids and sometimes they're in the garage. Had they seen the goods? I wasn't going to cop to it right there in the Dove bar aisle.

My heart is saying, "Hey, he's a neighbor with beautiful children, and he needs a little help. I should offer it."

"Yeah, we're really low too."

Walking out of the store, I rationalize my decision. I have a child in quarantine who had diarrhea yesterday. I have to think of him first, dammit. No one else is getting the Charmin. I go home and hide it.

Mikey is acting normally. No health issues with the other three. I am feeling more confident that he doesn't have the virus because he never had contact with someone contagious.

We've decided it was the two XL frappuccinos that stirred the pot.

MARCH 29: DAY 9

A friend of the family calls.

"Dave, I have to tell you something," Laura says too quietly. "My husband Greg has the virus."

"Oh no. I'm so sorry to hear that. Is he doing okay?"

"He is," she says. "But your Natalie was in our house last week so I thought I should tell you."

Pause.

"Okay. Well thanks so much for letting me know..."

Click.

"...that you gave us the plague."

Clearly our whole house is infected. Now I know where Mikey got it, from his sister. If he has it, how long before the rest of us?

"Natalie!"

"What's wrong?" she asks.

I tell her the news. "But I wasn't anywhere near her dad," she said.

"WebMD says that the evidence is pointing heavily toward aerosol transmission, and the particles may hang around for hours. Maybe you walked through some air-suspended particles."

"I feel fine. I don't think I have the virus, Dad. I think you're overreacting."

"I could be on a ventilator in a week! That's how I'm reacting," I say melodramatically, sans stage makeup.

Everything gets wiped down. I'm now distancing twenty-five feet from my daughter. As we're cleaning she asks me, "Dad, do you think we'll have a senior prom?"

Stop.

What an awful feeling. My little girl might not get to have a senior prom. Proms are unforgettable. I remember mine, the crème-beige tux with dark brown velour lapels, my bursting afro forming a chia-like circumference around my head. Irresistible.

The seniors need to have their prom. Everyone gets a senior prom. Except my brother John, who was sent back home after his date fell down drunk on the registration table.

"Honey, I hope they still have one," I tell Natalie. "Right now they should move it to at least mid-June." We should be out of the woods by then.

10:30 p.m.

I am informed by my oldest two that I need to stop wearing jeans all the time and have to get some joggers. The next ninety minutes of my life is spent online looking for joggers and I order a few pairs. Trying to stay away from those thigh-sucking slim ones. Guess we'll see.

MARCH 30: DAY 10

Sadlier Connect. That's the name of another learning platform the kids have to access to do this online schoolwork.

We are going to learn about idioms today. This should be fun since I haven't heard the word *idiom* in forty-one years. The Sadlier lesson states that students, "may have to recognize idioms on state tests." Which will be the last time students ever see that word in their lives.

"An idiom is a common word or phrase which means something different from its literal meaning, but can be understood because of its popular use."

Here's the question.

> Connor chose his best friend Alex to help him with his campaign for student council. The day before the election, Connor discovered that Alex had done nothing, and it dawned on him that he should have hitched his horse to a different wagon.
>
> Choose the answer that best describes the meaning of the idiom.
>
> a. When a person discovers that if you want a job done right, do it yourself
>
> b. When a person learns that it is your own responsibility for bad luck

c. When a person realizes that he could have made a better choice

d. When a person discovers that his friends may let him down

e. When a person loses all his friends for using phrases that stopped making sense in 1871 with the invention of the automobile

You hear the word *metaphor* all the time, which is idiom's cousin. A metaphor is a figure of speech where we compare one thing to another. But DON'T use like or as, because then it's a simile. Let's look at all three, shall we?

IDIOM

After 146 calls over a one-week remote period, Sam wanted to give those telemarketers a tall glass of COVID-19.

METAPHOR

The remote learning home was a frat house.

SIMILE

The kind father asked the mean principal not to tell everyone that he didn't know the answers to his daughter's third-grade quiz, but she spread it like COVID-19.

6:30 p.m.

I can't find Joey, but thought he was home. I have to call him, because that's what we do now. We call each other on cell phones inside a house.

"Where are you, Joe?"

"I'm downstairs in the basement," he says.

"I was just down there and you weren't there."

"I'm in the closet next to the furnace room," he responds.

"What are you doing in the closet?" I ask.

"Playing Xbox."

"Well, your Xbox isn't in the closet, Joe," I tell him. "It's by the TV."

"Yeah…well…I kind of set things up in here."

In the basement is a small walk-in closet where my beautiful wife wisely chose to keep our children's toys. The closet is four feet wide, ten feet long.

I walk downstairs and open the closet door. It looks like NASA. A large TV hooked to two computers. Some kind of battery-operated colored lights. An oversized beanbag was on the floor, squeezed wall to wall, functioning as a control chair-bed. On the shelf within eleven inches of reach were two cans of Dr. Pepper and a large container of Goldfish. On the floor under the TV was a microwave and a Keurig.

"Where'd you get a Keurig?" I ask.

"I found one in someone's garbage a few months ago and took it because it looked good. Still works."

"That's sanitary."

"I figured if I'm going to be stuck in the house, Dad, I may as well be creative," he says.

"Whatever. Just toss the Keurig and take the microwave out before we have a fire," I tell him.

I saw the space as three walls and a narrow closet. My son's 14-year-old eyes and imagination saw an entertainment center waiting to be developed.

I saw what it is. He saw what it could be.

Good lesson.

MARCH 31: DAY 11

Governor Pritzker announced today that he is extending the shelter-in-place order to April 30.

That should be enough reason for the airlines to cancel my flight, right? Wrong.

8:00 a.m.

My brother-in-law, Chris, dropped off a mask for me since you can't buy them anywhere. He's thoughtful. I went to the store and was going to wear the mask, but it wasn't the same as the other ones I had seen people wearing. Wasn't flat on my face. It looked like some kind of a dog muzzle, protruding out from my head. I kept the mask but didn't wear it much.

Today Brooke has math workbook pages. Takes me right back to Miss Clark, who must have been recruited from the juvey home. She'd snap, "All right now, take out your workbooks," and then crush us with problems. She once made us write, "I must not talk in class," one thousand times on loose-leaf paper. My friend Phil wanted to jam a potato in her car muffler.

Today's math problem from the workbook:

Allison bought 10 packages of energy bars. Each package contains 6 bars. Allison says she has a total of 65 bars. Is her answer reasonable?

Reasonable? What kind of a question is that? I don't know if it's reasonable. Is Allison on medication and unable to think clearly? Maybe then it would be reasonable.

The answer is no, Allison is wrong and if she doesn't even know her tens she has no business being out in the store buying treats. And why does she need sixty energy bars in the first place? Is Allison hung over?

Next problem. Common Core.

> Mr. Torres has some tomatoes. He arranges them in 3 rows and 8 columns. Draw a picture to represent this problem.

Really? This needs to be represented? Can't we just solve it? That's a lot of tomatoes to draw. I have a better idea. Why don't we draw a picture of a 3 and a picture of an 8 and tell you that it's 24 at harvest time?

12:30 a.m.

Brooke likes me to make up a story before bed every night. It's always the same one, where a new neighbor has moved in on our block. They are always special creatures who meet their demise at the end of the story so someone else can move in the next day.

We've had Goober Grape, Mush Banana, Mr. Pin, Wally Water Balloon, Good Ol' Charlie Pencilhead, Chuck Chapstick, Willy Wind, Harry Ham who later married Edna Egg, and a host of others.

Tonight is Crabby Carl Cornflake.

APRIL 1: DAY 12

A new month. The sun is out. Finally. We don't have spring here. We go from winter to mud.

I put a towel over my face and look into Mikey's room to see if he is breathing. It's hard to tell from twenty-seven feet away. I can't go closer but I think his foot moved. Good enough. I'll check on him later.

Towel immediately goes into the washing machine.

We should be done with the heavy snow so there is a ritual we have to abide by: draining the gas from the snowblower. I don't know how you're actually supposed to drain it so I let the snow blower run on the sidewalk for about two hours. Neighbors love it.

If you don't drain it and you leave it in all summer, it'll "gunk the fuel lines." That's what I learned last fall, the phrase, gunk the fuel lines.

My snowblower wouldn't start so I called the hardware store where I bought it and asked if they had any thoughts on why it wouldn't start.

"Did you drain the gas from the prior year?" he asked.

"I don't think I did."

"You left it in there all summer?" he queried in a Miss Clark tone.

"Well, I guess that would be the natural conclusion you could draw."

"You can't do that. You CANNOT leave gas in a snowblower all summer! You probably gunked the fuel lines."

"I'm sorry, I didn't mean to," I apologized. "What do I do now?"

Sighs. "Well, I suppose you can try changing the spark plug."

"I don't know how to do that. Is it hard?"

"No, it's pretty simple. You just take your socket wrench and then put the extender on and it should pop right off."

I don't know what a socket wrench is. My wife had tools; my son has tools. My father-in-law Glen has tools. I don't. I'm the only guy in the entire Home Depot store with a *Les Misérables* shirt.

It was the second lecture I had received on a snowblower that year. The prior winter I took it in and told the dealer it wasn't cleaning snow clearly off the driveway.

"Sounds to me, sir, like you have a problem with your auger," he said.

"My auger. And what would that be?"

"Sir, that's what feeds the snow to the blades. You probably damaged it by placing the snowblower directly on the driveway when you were snow blowing."

"Isn't that how you get the snow off the driveway?"

"No. Only use the snowblower if there's more than five inches of snow."

"Then how do I clear the driveway?" I asked.

"Use a shovel," he said seriously.

So that's why I take care of my snowblower now. After ninety minutes of it running, my children wake up ready to get at another day of learning from a distance.

2:00 p.m.

"Pop Bottle Project!

This means Dad has to go back to art class. I don't like construction paper, glue, any of that. Each student has to pick a person who has made a difference in the world. Then they have to create a model of that person out of a plastic pop bottle filled with rocks and sand.

Brooke picked Venus Williams. I hope she never finds out or sees this.

It's not due for a while, so we're going to put our little art project over on the side for a few weeks and enjoy the day.

Vocab for high school: Bibliophile. A lover of books.

That sounds a little creepy. Would you use that word? "Oh, there's my sweet Aunt Mary. She's a bibliophile, you know."

APRIL 2: DAY 13

I don't have to help the high school senior with her schoolwork. She gets it done.

To music. Music must be on at all times.

I never noticed it that much before because she's usually locked in her room. But during this home confinement, I hear it more.

Interesting lyrics, these rap songs. I can only make out about every fifth word. The one playing now sounds like they're saying pill popping and perc, apparently involving a girl named Molly. The singer is upset because someone took his drank. I don't know how you can take someone's drank. Then there is a reference to sucking, which is an obligatory inclusion in these tunes due to its rhyming potential.

I don't know what the song means, but I assume Molly needs an intervention.

We are onto another song quickly because my children are unable to listen to an entire song. Takes too long. This next melody is much more religious. He is thanking God that he does not have to smack a bitch today. It's always been the opening line to my prayers.

I've discovered a quirky little pattern in these songs. The singer complains about someone, then throws out eleven or twelve f-bombs, and that resolves the conflict.

This is different than when I was growing up. My mom shut off the song "Bad, bad, Leroy Brown, baddest man in the whole damn town...," because of the word damn. Thus my first reaction when I hear these lyrics is to shut it down. But then I'm the mean dad from *Footloose*.

When I see them listening to music, they're happy. Science and health experts tell us that music releases endorphins in the brain, and that lowers anxiety and can even help the immune system.

Children today are under intense pressure to excel, to exceed expectations, more so than at any time before. Layer in a frightening health crisis and a complete upheaval of their lives without anyone having a good explanation for what to expect, and I'm good with music that brings them a smile.

But they do get a mini-lecture about those lyrics and the constant f-bombs. George Cullen, my friend Mike's dad, used to say, "If you can't come up with a better word than a swear word, you're not very smart. In fact you're a dumbass."

I told Natalie that and she said, "Yeah but don't you think those swear words really fit well when you're mad about something, like when you jammed your toe the other night, Dad?" Smart a-a-a-leck.

Brooke's work today includes a writing assignment on diamante poems. This is in the Scott Foresman Readers and Writers Notebook. This poem style was "invented" forty years ago by some guy.

I'm sure all of you at home know what a diamante poem is, but as a refresher for myself, here is the description.

The diamante poem has seven lines, the first and last have nouns with opposite meanings, second and sixth lines have adjectives, third and fifth lines have verbs, and fourth has four nouns.

Example in the book.

Plants
Leafy, healthy
Watering, feeding, growing
Garden, yards, forests, jungles
Running, hunting, surviving
Brave, wild
Animals

Now the students are to write one. Maybe:

Molly
Popping Pills
Pop Hop Stop
Song, Intervention, Jail, Record
Suck Smack Pray
God

Perhaps I'm in the wrong frame of mind to help with this today.

APRIL 3: DAY 14

"Dad, who was Judas, again?" Brooke asks.

"He's the one responsible for giving all of mankind guilt. But his character got a terrific role in an Andrew Lloyd Webber musical."

We are studying a little religion today as we get closer to Easter. Joe is finding it a bit repetitive. "I've been learning the same thing for nine years," he says. "Wouldn't it be better if everyone had to know, really know, all the religions? Isn't that why there are so many wars?"

"Yep. Walk in someone else's shoes, you understand where they're coming from," I say.

"What if their shoes are smelly?" Brooke asks.

We learn the most from walking in smelly shoes. Then you know what's causing the stink.

12:30 p.m.

The New York COVID numbers today: ten thousand new cases in one day. Another 562 deaths. The death rate doubled in three days. A shortage of ventilators.

In Illinois another 1209 new cases, fifty-three more deaths—the biggest jump in one day on both counts. McCormick Place, a massive convention center on Lake Michigan named after a descendant of the man who invented the reaper, was being transformed into a hospital. These transformations are happening in major cities across the country.

I keep thinking about these doctors and nurses and what must be going through their minds every day. These are the individuals who choose to spend their time on Earth, taking care of the rest of us on the planet. I think about my nephew Bobby, an emergency room doctor in Texas who was heartbroken when they couldn't save a child from the virus. I think about his sister Lindsay, a nurse in New York, and her husband Mike, trying to protect their firstborn child. We all have friends or family in this profession. Sheltering in place doesn't keep it from hitting home.

Maybe we all need a little religion right now.

APRIL 4: DAY 15

I feel like something is stuck in my throat. Been going on for months. Two doctors have said it's probably some stress condition. Please, what could be causing stress? The virus or the fact that we lose one sock in every laundry cycle? THAT'S what should trigger that washing machine jingle, when it locates a missing sock!

Today is the gastroenterologist. Because I also have a cervical disc pain, I've self-diagnosed through extensive Google research that the cervical disc C-6 is protruding into my throat.

I found another guy in a different country who had this condition. Surgery likely.

Did the virtual meeting with the gastro and informed him of my diagnosis and the various ailments. After I speak non-stop for about twenty minutes, he asks, "Have you ever tried Xanax?"

***

One hour after being informed that I should be sedated, Natalie says to me, "Dad, did you see Mikey's eyes?"

Nothing coming after a question like that can be good.

"What's wrong with his eyes?" I ask.

"They're all red. Maybe he has pink eye."

On to WebMD, and there it is:

WEDNESDAY, April 1, 2020 (HealthDay News) -- Besides causing COVID-19, the new coronavirus can also lead to pink eye..."

His eyes are red but I can't tell if they're bloodshot or if it's pink eye. I'd be relieved if he'd been on a bender.

Called the pediatrician and he told me that his office doesn't even have COVID tests yet. He said, "It's hard to say if Mikey has the virus based upon those symptoms, but you never know, he could have it."

He could have it. Just enough to traumatize. I can't blame the doctor. He doesn't have a test and honestly doesn't know.

So Mikey's back in the penalty box and Dad's wondering about the upside to Xanax.

APRIL 5: DAY 16

Big day. First pair of joggers arrived. I try them on for Natalie.

"Where'd you get those?" she asks.

"Amazon. You like them?"

"They're shiny," she says, smirking. "What material is that?"

"I don't know. The product description said they were comfortable and got four stars."

"Who even makes those?" she asks, pounding away at my purchase.

"I don't know. Some Amazon brand. Should I return them?"

"Well, are you going to wear them outside?"

"That's usually the plan with clothes, but I think you've answered my questions on this pair. Back they go."

***

Easter is a week away. I ask Brooke what she wants from the Easter Bunny.

"Is he still coming?" she asks.

"Oh, definitely. Bunnies can't get the virus," I explain.

"I want some hoo-hoo markers."

Jesus, whatever that is it doesn't sound like something from the Easter Bunny.

"I'm sorry, honey, what did you want?" I ask.

"Hoo-hoo markers."

That's what I thought I heard. "Honey, can you show me on Amazon what you're talking about?"

She showed me. "Oh, they're called Ohuhu markers, I see."

What the hell kind of a name is that for children's markers? "Is there anything else you want from the Easter Bunny?" I ask.

"Yes, oobleck."

I'm on a roll. "Oobleck? Daddy doesn't know what that means, sweetie."

"That's what it's called, Dad. It's called oobleck," she says.

Joey walks in during this and, finally, I get a little help. "It's slime. It's a package of slime."

I look it up and it's this gooey liquid and solid substance named after a Dr. Seuss book, *Bartholomew and the Oobleck*. As the story goes, King Derwin of Didd had his magicians mutter the following quoted incantation to make this stuff.

Oh, snow and rain are not enough!
Oh, we must make some brand-new stuff!
So feed the fire with wet mouse hair, burn and onion. Burn a chair.
Burn a whisker from your chin and burn a long sour lizard skin
...Go make the oobleck tumble down on every street, in every town!
~Dr. Suess

Definitely a product you want in the home.

Bartholomew Cubbins helped save the Didd kingdom, which was being destroyed by the oobleck. He got the king to say, "I'm sorry, this was all my fault." Those words were magical and brought out the sun and dried up the oobleck.

Heartwarming. But it's never sunny here. Not in April, not in May. And now the Easter Bunny is bringing oobleck to our house.

APRIL 6: DAY 17

I hate these Chromebooks. These are awful little computers. They don't have the backspace delete button and you have to squish your fingers on the cursor to move it.

The Sadlier Connect has our seventh grade working on antonyms. The question is to find the word from the list provided that means the opposite of an honest person. It's not there. There are perhaps one hundred antonyms that Sadlier could have used, but didn't. There is no word in the list that is an antonym for an honest person.

I'm growing impatient because I have to scroll up and down repeatedly to check the list of potential antonyms. I'm half-yelling at a twelve-year-old, "Scroll down, SCROLL DOWN, I CAN'T SEE THE ANTONYMS, MIKEY!"

That's not normal. I then do what any rational parent would do. I call the principal. Teachers love it when parents let them know that the book is wrong.

"Hey, Margaret, I just wanted to let you know that on the seventh-grade antonym assignment, there's no good answer for number five."

"What?"

"Sadlier Connect lesson for today, there's no antonym in the list for 'honest person,'" I say.

"It's there," she says in the principal tone. They all have a tone. "I'm sure it's there."

"No, it's not," I say. "I'm looking at the assignment, it's not there."

"Well, maybe you should just let Mikey do the assignment," she says.

"I'm helping him," I say.

"Yeah, well, you're obviously not doing a very good job with it, are you?" she says, chuckling. "Looks like you're still having problems with seventh-grade work."

She'll tell every teacher in the school about our call. Then she'll call the ones who have retired. It won't end.

APRIL 7: DAY 18

"Have you heard any more about Natalie's prom?" Leona asks in a morning call.

"No, we still don't know," I tell her. "They're talking about mid-May, but I think they'll have to go into the summer."

"They better have one. I spent $450 on that friggin' dress. She looks gorgeous in it."

Yes, she does. Leona bought the dress for Natalie, a beautiful gift. The woman works nonstop to give nice things to her grandchildren.

"All those kids on the block might not get a prom. That's terrible," she says.

It's true. Ashley, Clarissa, Michael, Christian, Maggie and Rosie— children I have watched grow up, are all being told they might not get a senior prom.

Then there's the other question: "What's next? Where are you going to college?" People take it a step further and ask, "What does she want to do after college?" She doesn't know. Should any seventeen-year-old? Every child has a talent and all we can do is plant the seed of courage for them to use it.

In my adult lifetime, someone came up with this concept called "touring" the college. You travel hundreds of miles and spend a day walking around the campus looking at the buildings. They all have an Administration building, often a reddish-color brick. A fountain, workout building, the thirty-seven buildings where they have classes, eateries, and dorms.

I can hear my father's words, "Why don't you just read about the school and see what it offers for what you'd like to study?" Can't do that, Dad, because that would be free. Have to experience it. Visualize it to satisfy the Common Core element of life.

The irony, not to be confused with simile or idiom, is that this has become the norm even though we can see pretty much the same thing in a video tour.

We were able to get in one tour before the virus hit. Two full days alone, just Natalie and me—traveling, laughing, a little rap (still hate it), and an excellent, informative tour.

I wish I could do fifty of them.

APRIL 8: DAY 19

Citations. How to properly cite an author's work. You cannot graduate from high school until you have suffered through this wretched process.

This is worse than learning the metric and Dewey Decimal systems.

You've got the MLA Handbook published by the Modern Language Association that's used for humanities, such as English, history, or drama.

There's the APA Manual published by the American Psychological Association for the science and education fields. I can understand why the psychology department is involved with this one because of what it does to someone's head.

Next, we have the Chicago Manual of Style, which by title alone sounds impressive. This is published by the University of Chicago Press, and you can use it for anything, although historical footnotes are their specialty.

A fourth is the AP style from the Associated Press, popular for journalists.

If you're writing a title under APA or AP, then for every word that has four letters or more you capitalize the first letter. If your flavor is Chicago or MLA, never forget that all prepositions are lowercase. And shouldn't they be, for heaven's sake?

For APA, use quotations for a song or journal title, but underline or italicize books. For AP never italicize or underline a book; use quotations. But for Chicago use quotations for articles and chapter titles, but italicize books. Italicize books and websites for MLA, but quotes go around songs and articles.

And then the lead character in most grammar horror films, the Oxford comma. This is the last comma when you write a list of three or more things. Chicago, MLA, and APA all say use it, like I did in this sentence. Don't even think about using one under AP, unless the meaning of the sentence would be destroyed without it.

Now, if you have a quotation of four or more lines then you must set it off on a new line indented one inch if you're using MLA; but not under APA, because that calls for quotes of forty words or more to be set off and indented a half-inch; which is different than Chicago, where quotations of one hundred words or more should be set off as block quotes and indented using the Tab key once.

Don't forget the APA change in 2019, where they recommend adding an apostrophe and an *s*—rather than an apostrophe alone—to form the possessive of names that end in an unpronounced *s*.

Here's what I'm thinking. You know how some guy invented the diamante poem? I could invent "Dave's Rules of Citations," where, as long you say who wrote it and what page, you're good to go.

APRIL 9: DAY 20

I don't understand the lives of these people in the math problems.

1. Clay learned that solids have a definite shape. Now he wants to measure the mass of a bead.

He wants to measure the mass of a bead? Of a bead? Why, why do you want to do that, Clay?

2. Harrison has a 40-liter fish tank. How many 4-centimeter fish can he put in his fish tank?

Is he going to put water in the tank or just squeeze a thousand fish in there? And Harrison is measuring his pet fish? He should call Clay. They could do an entire routine on volume.

1:30 p.m.

"Dad, I need to go to the Dollar Store," Brooke says.

"Why?"

"Because I need foam board for my art project."

"I'm not going to the Dollar Store. You don't need foam board."

"Yes, I do, I doooo, Dad," comes the whine. "My teacher said we need foam board for the project. I need it to make Venus Williams's head."

"I'm sure she'd be flattered that you want her head to be foam. Use a golf ball, but not a Pro V," I tell her.

"I can't use a golf ball, Dad! That's too heavy. It'll fall off the bottle."

"If it falls off during your presentation, say she was martyred. Half of those people had their heads cut off anyway."

4:30 p.m.

Natalie's friend Sarah calls, the one whose dad almost gave us the virus. She was in tears.

"Natalie....Natalie...you have to tell me something, okay?" she cries.

"Oh my God, what is it, is everyone okay? Is your dad okay?" Natalie asks.

"He's fine...but you are, like, my closest friend, and I am going to ask you something, and you need to swear that you'll tell me the truth," she says.

"I will, I will, I promise. What is it??"

"Do I have a really big forehead?"

And people with the virus think they have worries.

"Of course not. What are you talking about?" Natalie asks her.

"This guy...this guy was walking past me in the store and said, "Jeez, you really have a huge forehead."

See, now that's the guy who needs to get the virus.

7:30 p.m.

It's Holy Thursday. Erica and her mom used to drive around and visit churches on this night, a tradition many follow. Not this year. Whatever your faith, it's hard when the churches are dark.

APRIL 10: DAY 21

The schoolwork is light. Last day before Easter break. Last day for the airline to come to their senses and cancel my first-class flight, but they don't, of course. Erica's brother Gary told me it's what I deserve for flying that "other" airline. He's a dispatcher for United.

11:00 a.m.

Vocabulary today includes the word *prodigious*. Prodigious: Impressively great in extent or size.

Use in a sentence:

The rude man with a nanoscopic face told the girl she had a prodigious forehead.

9:30 p.m.

Off to Mariano's. This is when I like to go because most of the infected are sleeping.

By 9:45, I'm in the cookie aisle facing the back of the store. I put two packages of chocolate chip cookies in the cart because these are known to fight coronaviruses. I look up and freeze.

The guys are bringing in crates of toilet paper.

It is like seeing the Emerald City.

I look around, as if I am meeting a heroin dealer, and approach the man bringing in the supplies. The toilet paper is still in large boxes, and then those boxes are wrapped tightly in cellophane, apparently having been delivered by a Brink's truck.

"Excuse me, can I possibly get a package of toilet paper from one of the boxes?" I ask.

"Well, sir, we haven't unpacked it yet and we're supposed to put it on the shelf first."

A woman walks up and overhears this. She isn't having any part of it.

"I don't think so," she says. "This store is closing in eight minutes and I need this now."

She rips open the cellophane and takes a package of toilet paper. The delivery man walks away, sighing, "I don't care. Do whatever you want."

Sounds like permission to me. But I'm not going to take just any package. You can only buy one, so I need a Charmin 24 = 96 Ultra Strong. None there at six minutes until closing time, so I'm forced to go with the 12 = 48s.

One thought goes through my head on the way home: I know the day and time they deliver toilet paper. Do I tell people? I say one word and it gets out, it's over.

I'll say nothing. I put it discreetly in the back of the car and head out into the night.

APRIL 11: DAY 22

"Coronavirus Ravages Nursing Homes, Killing Thousands."

That's the headline.

It isn't fair. Not the people who can't help themselves. Not the families who feel terrible that a loved one is even in a nursing home.

One year ago, my mom, Therese, was in one. She had fallen and needed rehab with around-the-clock nursing care. She never complained and had a smile for every soul, because she knows no other way. The staff was wonderful under very trying circumstances. The food...no words. I'm sure those in starving countries might occasionally like it.

Every night that you walk out of a nursing care facility leaving your mom or dad behind, is gut-wrenching. Whenever we needed them, they were always at our side.

I cannot imagine being told that the virus is in the nursing home, but you can't go in. That you can't rescue someone you love from the proverbial fire.

That's what happened to a friend. Then came the call that her dad had the virus and was being taken to the hospital. But she couldn't go in the ICU room. "Try to FaceTime," they told her.

Saying goodbye through a screen. That's the COVID-19 virus.

My mom made it out of that nursing home in 2019. Though her memory isn't what it was, she never forgets to smile, never forgets to see only the best in every person. She has a caretaker in her home. Kind woman from the Philippines. Her English isn't very good and much of the time I don't know what she's saying.

She texts me when she needs groceries. Sometimes she'll send along a picture of the item so that I understand. Today she sent me a text which said "bananas" under a picture of Comet.

Maybe I should get my mom some takeout from the nursing home.

APRIL 12, EASTER SUNDAY: DAY 23

The Easter Bunny came! Can't believe he found the Ohuhu markers. He didn't have the same luck with the oobleck, because the children of the kingdom hadn't learned how to say, "I'm wrong, Dad"—the magic words to control the gooey substance.

10:00 a.m.

We watch Easter Sunday mass on television. A priest saying mass to an empty church on Easter is another sad first. Joey and Brooke goof off during the service to remain consistent with their standard church behavior.

We didn't go to California, but at least it's been nice here. Over sixty-five degrees for two straight days. We have two magnolia trees in the backyard. When it blooms, it's absolutely beautiful. We can see that it's starting to bloom. The white flowers will be coming in this week.

Joe decides to put on a full-on Easter Bunny costume and hop through the backyards of neighbors without saying anything to them. My next-door neighbor Jordan said she was out in the back, saw a big (non-Easter-like adjective) paw on top of her gate, and ran back in the house.

Still no fever or virus for Mikey. Good news.

APRIL 13: DAY 24

I didn't think we had any schoolwork over break. We do if the work from last week wasn't completed. Mikey didn't finish social studies. His assignment included reading about Lord Baltimore, who was the founder of the colony of Maryland. He was a Catholic, so he wanted to make Maryland a Catholic colony. Isn't that always the case with us Catholics?

Lord B. wanted government to allow for religious freedom, so an act was passed, with an opening paragraph that says:

> Be it therefore ordered and enacted by the Right Honorable Cecilius Lord Baron of Baltimore, Absolute Lord and Proprietary of this Province...

Right, Honorable, Lord, Baron, Absolute Lord and Proprietary of the Province. Yes, right, but who is in charge?

This act says that if you utter reproachful words about the Virgin Mary, the Apostles, or Evangelists, you shall be "publicly whipped."

If you profane the Sabbath by "frequent swearing or drunkenness," you get fined. Third offense, you get whipped.

To preserve "mutual love and amity," among citizens, if you disturb or trouble someone based upon their belief in Jesus, or interfere with their religion, you owe them money. If you don't pay up, you get whipped.

Finally, those that blaspheme Jesus or the Holy Trinity are punished with death.

They called this the Maryland Act of Toleration.

APRIL 14: DAY 25

It snowed overnight. The magnolia flowers are dead. I can't even see the dead white petals that fell off the trees because the ground is so white. I tell my sister in California about our snow.

"Yeah, it's 78 here today," Di says. "Supposed to be sunny and warm all week."

"That's nice. I'm going to shovel because I already drained all the gas out of the snowblower," I tell her.

"We can't go anywhere, so we're just going to sit by the pool," she says, quickly adding, "in the warm sun."

"Should be really warm there when the wildfires start up again," I say, unable to resist. The virus is making me a bitter pill.

6:00 p.m.

The Republicans and Democrats are fighting more, each side blaming the other for something related to the coronavirus.

It's nothing new. Today marks 155 years since President Lincoln was shot and killed by John Wilkes Booth because Booth disagreed with Lincoln's politics.

History has a lesson for us in there.

APRIL 15: DAY 26

"Dad, can we get a dog?" Brooke asks.

"No."

"Why not? Don't you like dogs?"

"I love dogs, but you guys won't take care of it, and I have enough responsibilities right now."

"I will take care of it," she assures me. "I promise I'll walk it every day and I have a lot of time right now because I'm home."

"Right, but what happens when you go to school, honey?"

"We'll get one of those dogs that doesn't have to go as much."

"That's called a cat."

"Oh, come on, Dad, please."

"You can't even take care of a washcloth, and you want a dog?"

"What about a wiener dog?" she asks. "I think they're cute."

Joe hears this and decides to chime in. "Let's get a dog and name it *Dammit*. 'Come 'ere, Dammit!'"

"Any excuse to swear, Joe," I say. "Any way you can sneak one in."

This is the anniversary of the date the Titanic sank in 1912. It is said that in every tragedy of this magnitude, we learn valuable lessons. One often cited from the Titanic sinking is that we need to make sure we always have appropriate personal protection in the event of an unforeseen emergency that could take lives.

Good thing we learned that one.

APRIL 16: DAY 27

Mikey is complaining that his sisters won't get out of the bathroom. "They've been in there for two hours!" he says.

"Can't you use another one?" I ask him.

"No. I want that one. That's where my stuff is."

Two hours isn't good. "Natalie, open the door, please," I ask. At that moment, there were perhaps one thousand responses that wouldn't have surprised me.

"Dad, Brooke and I have lice." That wasn't one of them.

"Are you kidding me?" I ask.

"No, we really have it. We snuck out to Nane's yesterday to have her do the treatment," Natalie says, using the kids' term of endearment for their grandmother Leona.

How? How is it possible to be quarantined, sheltered in place, six feet from every other human for a month, and get lice?

This is the wretched in-school plague that is spread by some kid who doesn't wash his hair and then gives it to your child. Every parent knows this. It doesn't start with our children. You find out your child has lice, you blame another kid in school along with his parents, the principal, and the school board. A dirty little kid gave my angel lice.

What am I supposed to think now? That my children are the originators of a lice condition? Are those sticky little hair grubs in my house?

Natalie and Brooke are doing those nauseating lice treatments where you run that tiny comb with white cream through each strand of hair to make sure you get every living thing off your scalp.

I loathe little bugs, rodents, snakes, lizards, any kind of crawly things. Joe tells me they're all part of the food chain. Lice are not part of the food chain unless something eats your head.

I Google it.

"Lice can live for thirty days on the human head....Females can lay six eggs a day. However, they cannot jump or fly." That's reassuring, that we don't have flying lice.

APRIL 17: DAY 28

Natalie comes running downstairs, all excited. We don't see that often because she received all the German genes.

There will be a senior prom in July. I am so happy for my little girl.

She calls Leona. "Nane, guess what? We're going to have prom in July!"

Leona starts crying. She cries easily. "Oh, honey, I am so happy for you," she says. "I want to see you wear that friggin' dress we bought."

It is a beautiful dress. I don't know where the other half of it is, but I am told, "That's what everybody's wearing." Time to shut up, Dad.

"Did you get the shampoo?" Leona asks me.

"Yes, we got it, thanks." She has a special shampoo that hairdressers use for lice.

"Have the girls use that for about two weeks. That'll kill the lice."

"I may use it because my head has been itchy since they told me," I say.

"Then you use it too. It won't hurt you. Anyway, I'm so happy Natalie gets to go to a prom… You know, I've decided I'm never retiring. I can't stand sitting around all day. I cleaned every closet in the house….And that's it. That's it."

The lice-killing shampoo is a thick, green, pungent goo. I think it's oobleck. I put it in my hair and I may as well have put my head in the fireplace. There is this intense burning compression of the skull, apparently targeting lice which have burrowed deep into the brain.

APRIL 18: DAY 29

I have a neighbor who works for the federal government. I can't use his real name in this book, because he's in a high-ranking position. I don't want to compromise that in any way. I'll call him moT.

He gets the scoop on what's coming down from Washington. The real story. I love being out in front of the house talking with him. I can always tell when I'm going to get the dirt because he pauses and then looks up and down the block before he starts with the heavy stuff. I'm guessing he's checking for disguised surveillance trucks picking up our audio. Could be a gaggle of feds in the back of an Amazon truck for all I know.

I like to start by giving him a softball question.

"So how's it going at work?"

He looks around. No Amazon trucks. "So what stores have you been to since the shutdown?" he asks me.

"Hardly any," I tell him. "Grocery store, gas station, that's about it."

"Exactly."

The moment begged for musical underscoring as the plot thickened.

"If the bad guys know everyone is only going to certain stores, what happens?" he says.

Hmm. They take the toilet paper? I never guess the ending of movies right, so I wasn't sure. "What happens?" I ask.

"They get hit," he says.

"By who?"

"Same people who like to attack our country. Terrorists. Not saying it would happen. Just be careful."

He takes a long drag of a cigarette, looks around, flips the cigarette butt, and walks back to his house.

He doesn't smoke actually, but that would be a better ending.

APRIL 19: DAY 30

Uncle John calls from Phoenix to check on Mikey. My brother can raise someone's blood pressure in under four seconds.

He once called a helicopter rental agency and asked them, in a recorded call, if he could rent a helicopter to drop boxes of wet newspapers on his neighbor's house.

Today he is checking on Mikey and encouraging him to stretch out any illness a minimum of three weeks.

2:30 p.m.

Natalie and Joey were out driving around, stopping at whatever stores were open to kill time. When they get home, Joey jumps out of the car with this huge smile.

"Dad, look what I found at Walgreens." He holds up a small package of four rolls of toilet paper.

"Good eyes, Joey!" I tell him.

The things that make a father proud during a remote learning isolation. He tosses me the package and, after recovering from the thought that the plastic packaging may not have been wiped down in compliance with Dr. Gupta standards, I noticed that it was single-ply.

Single-ply toilet paper is too thin. It's like camping. I'm not a camper. I like to camp in places that have pools and a nice building with plush beds where you can sleep. I understand how people like to be at one with nature, but nature also has bugs. And bears. If there's a bear in my hotel room, it's free.

I can't tell Joey that he grabbed the wrong kind of toilet paper. I could scar him for life. No, instead, I'll stay positive that he took the initiative to identify a need and satisfy it, along with satisfying his need for six canisters of sour cream and onion Pringles.

It was a memorable spring break. Snow, lice, and single-ply toilet paper. Tomorrow we're back.

APRIL 20: DAY 31

It's 1:00 in the afternoon and they're all asleep. It's probably better that they don't see my frustration with having to help with Common Core math again.

USE STRATEGIES TO MULTIPLY

Alfredo has three bags of oranges in each hand. Each bag contains five oranges. How many oranges does Alfredo have?

Use structure to solve. Look for relationships when using counters, drawings, skip counting, arrays, or known facts to solve the problem.

Do we need to have a relationship with the oranges? He has fifteen in each hand. Assuming he has two hands, we're at thirty. Do we need to draw thirty little orange circles? And who buys thirty oranges at one time? Maybe Alfredo knows they're out of Vitamin C at all the stores.

COMMON CORE ASSESSMENT

Write a multiplication story for 6 x 4. Draw a picture to represent the story. Then solve.

This all seems very personal, the animated story about a 6 and 4, the relationships of an orange. Who knew there was so much to think about?

The Story of 6 and 4

Dave, a pleasant and patient father who hates bugs, had four children. Each one received six Common Core math assignments during a pandemic. If Dave required one Xanax for each Common Core assignment, how many total did he take during e-learning classes?

6:30

Got a call from my friend Dave. Been the best of friends since we were four years old. He was just checking in and we laughed a lot. We need that. We need more of that today.

APRIL 21: DAY 32

What is it like in other homes?

I wonder what other parents are saying to their kids during this. Do they have a nice set time to do the work and then talk through it to make sure that their child is learning? Maybe they go for a walk and then have a nice healthy celery snack.

Yeah, not here. There haven't been any of those days. And the nights are getting worse.

Natalie sent me a picture from last evening's activities. My fifteen and twelve-year-old sons decided to take a bath in the kitchen sink, each sitting in one side, piled in bubbles of dish soap.

I can't get upset about it. Those were the biggest smiles I've seen on my boys in a month. Maybe I'll try it later.

11:30 a.m.

Brooke calls her grandpa Glen on FaceTime. She misses him, as we all do. He loves to stop by and see the kids, but he hasn't been here for a month. His lungs are compromised and he can't take that chance. How the virus separates. I see his eyes light up when he is talking to her. Just like Leona's, just like Erica's. So much is said in one look.

1:00

Third-grade science question:

Name three habits of a frog.

No, YOU name three habits of a frog. I don't know any. Are they drinkers?

At some point a committee of very bright people made a decision on what material would make the final edition of this science book so that the children of the world could be educated. They sat at a big, round table:

"I have one we can use," a committee member says. "Name one habit of a frog."

"Oh that's good, that's really good, Herbert," the others say, fawning.

"Wait, wait, I have an even better one. Name three habits of a frog!"

"Winner! We are done with page 25!"

2:30 p.m.

High school biology.

I'm not good at this. My biology teacher, Brother MacDonald, wrote on my exam, "Heilmann, you just make these theories up! Stay away from science!!!" True story.

Today's chapter covers T lymphocytes, which many don't care to know about.

But we should.

Lymphocytes are white blood cells that help us fight viruses, infections, and cancer. The T stands for the thymus, a gland that sits in the top of the chest and does most of its work when you're a child. The thymus gland has a hormone called thymosin, which helps stimulate the development of these T lymphocytes, or T cells.

There are these guys called "killer" T cells. When we are first infected with a virus or bacteria, they destroy those infected cells so the disease doesn't spread. Then they remember that invader and help our immune system fight it off if it ever comes around again. It's like having a dog that bites burglars or people who cough in your face.

Most people I know go through life never hearing about that gland, the thymus. It meant nothing to me—until it meant everything. Cancer of the thymus.

Science is not my strong suit, but I'm thankful for every teacher who brings this to children. One of those students will use that foundation to discover the vaccine that will stop this virus and put an end to extended remote learning.

10:00 p.m.

I don't understand why there is so much laundry. They wear clothes for twenty minutes and bang, down the laundry chute. Won't hang it back up.

I'm frustrated because I use those little pods for the washer and a few broke and they were all stuck together. I had the bright idea of running a little warm water on them and the pods thought they were in the washing machine. So we're done for the night.

APRIL 22: DAY 33

The last three weeks, when I wake up and walk, it feels like someone has beaten my heels while I was sleeping. I have self-diagnosed plantar fasciitis.

I'm reminded of my friend's fraternity where they spread the basement floor with Wheaties, then blindfolded the pledge class, brought them down, broke a few bottles nearby, and shouted, "NOW WALK ON THE GLASS, WALK ON THE GLASS!!" The eighteen-year-olds would walk on Wheaties screaming like a dad using Common Core math. Cruel, but a little funny.

Anyhow, I bought a pair of gym shoes that provide "orthotic support." Natalie told me that it looks like I still have the shoebox on my foot.

4:00 p.m.

Joe is done with his schoolwork and wants to drive a little. He's fifteen and has his learner's permit. My neighbor Maura saw him backing out and said I should take him over to the cemetery, where she was taught. She learned on a stick and popped the clutch into a tombstone. Said her mom wore a construction helmet and held rosary beads in the car. I don't know if she ever measured the mass of the beads, like Clay.

The patron saint of automobile drivers is Saint Frances of Rome, who died in 1440, just before the car was invented in 1885.

10:00 p.m.

Illinois had 2,049 new COVID-19 infections today, with another 98 deaths. Governor Pritzker will announce tomorrow that the shelter-in-place order will be extended to May 30, with a requirement that masks be worn in public.

APRIL 23: DAY 34

I lost my friend Pauly today. Not sure why we kept calling him Pauly as an adult, but it fit.

God, he made me laugh.

Pauly used to sell mattresses. Back then, he was 5'10", 384 pounds, or "damn near four spins" as he would describe himself, referring to the spinning dial when he stepped on a scale. At work, Pauly would jump on the beds in front of customers and say, "Holds up well, doesn't it?"

I loved a story he shared of when he was little, and he went camping with his older brother John. They were toasting marshmallows.

"John, that last marshmallow is mine. You had all yours."

"No, Paul. I'm eating it."

"John, I swear to God, you take that marshmallow and I'm setting your hair on fire."

"I'm taking it, Paul."

"It's MINE, JOHN!"

John ate the marshmallow.

I asked, "What did you do?"

"I took my stick, placed it in the fire, and then set his hair on fire."

"My mom got reeallly mad."

Remembering his funny stories helps to lift. That's what humor does.

2:00 p.m.

Mikey's teacher announces that they will be learning *Romeo and Juliet* next week.

Today, April 23, is Shakespeare's birthday. It's also the day Erica and I were engaged. On the stage of Shakespeare's Globe Theatre in London, in 1999.

It replays over and over in my head. And in a broken heart.

APRIL 24: DAY 35

The local politicians have decided that masks are now mandatory. My neighbor, moT has an N95 from work, because of his job.

An N95. It's like the kid on the block with the shiny new toy. If he walks outside his house with the mask, all the other dads would be jealous.

Except my neighbor two doors down, Gary. He'd say, "You don't need an N95, whatever the hell that means. Take it off, you big baby!" He tells it like it is, no b.s. Good south-sider.

These masks are so in demand that companies are selling knock-offs. I looked it up and the website I find says:

> "Charlatans rarely miss a chance to take advantage of a crisis, and that's presently playing out amidst the COVID-19 pandemic. People are selling counterfeit N95 respirators, warns the US Centers for Disease Control and Prevention (CDC)."

Charlatans? The warning begins with the word *charlatans*? Are we in 1897? I'll bet the rapscallions are coming next for Ma's horse.

The article continues:

> "You can tell at a glance which N95s are counterfeit. The real McCoys are clearly marked as being approved by the National Institute for Occupational Safety and Health (NIOSH)."

The real McCoys. If I used that phrase to the almost-college student, I'd get the stare.

So the website ticks off all the warning signs for a fake mask, such as not having the proper NIOSH stamp on the mask. Another giveaway is when NIOSH is misspelled NISH. Because wearing a NISH is like wearing nothing at all.

There was a picture on the website of an N95. It looked familiar. I went to my car and looked at the mask my brother-in-law had given me.

An N95. I have an N95! Those charlatans didn't get me. I can't wait to go to the store.

APRIL 25: DAY 36

Illinois has its highest number of new cases in a 24-hour period: 2,724. Another 108 deaths. Total cases in Illinois are now more than 36,000. Some states are talking of reopening at the end of the month.

Meanwhile, back at the computer, there is a more pressing world history question:

How did the Edict of Nantes affect the Huguenots?

Well, hopefully it got them to be better dressers. Those ruffled shirts with the long hose, good heavens. If any group needed a Lululemon.

Anyway, back in the 1500s in France, there were religious wars between the Catholic majority and the French Protestants, who were called the Huguenots. Don't ask me where they came up with that one. Henry IV took the throne in 1589—as I'm sure you know—and even though he converted to Catholicism, he wanted peace. The Edict of Nantes helped stop the vicious religious wars and granted the Protestants religious toleration.

His goal was to bring together a divided country and "put a chicken in every pot on Sunday."

And I'll bet you thought that "chicken in every pot" line came from the campaign of President Herbert Hoover.

Interesting approach Henry took, wasn't it? He was King and yet chose to reach across the aisle and give the minority much of what they wanted. To bring peace. Interesting lesson, that is.

APRIL 26: DAY 37

Taking a cue from Henry, I decide to have a chicken for dinner since it's Sunday. I send Natalie to the store, and she comes home with two fresh chickens.

"Everyone has a mask on at the store. They all look ridiculous. Actually, a friend of mine works behind the meat counter, so we talked for a few minutes. He said a guy who works at the store, his wife has the virus, but he keeps coming to the store."

"What department does he work in?" I ask.

"The meat counter."

Great. Has this guy touched all the chickens? Someone has to put them on that pan that goes on display. The pans are metal. The virus can live on metal for days.

I Googled it. High cooking temperatures likely kill the virus. The SARS virus, which is close to COVID-19, is inactivated at 132-149 degrees. Set bake temp to 350.

7:30 p.m.

Leona calls Natalie. I'm trying to ignore the FaceTime conversation, but it's a little loud.

"Natalie, I'm watching *The Avengers* and I don't understand who any of these people are."

"Nane, you're watching the fifth movie in the series. You have to watch them in order to understand the backstories," Natalie explains.

"I don't want to do that. I paused the movie so I could call you and figure this out. How can they all hold hands and just blast into space?"

"That's the power they have, Nane. You should watch them in order."

"They live in space?"

"No. They don't live in space."

"Then I'm turning it off because I don't know what the hell they're doing," Leona says. "And that's it. That's it."

APRIL 27: DAY 38

It's been fifty-four days since my last haircut. If I have lice, I don't know how they'll get out.

I sit on a lounge chair and quickly sense a prickly feeling on my backside from something I sat on. It is Brooke's hairbrush. It appears deformed.

"Brooke, is this your hairbrush?"

"Oh, yeah. We tried to boil that one to get the lice off and it kind of melted. I put it on the chair because I didn't know where else to put it."

Well, up my --- wasn't an option.

Today's third-grade lesson is subject pronouns, object pronouns, and possessive pronouns. Brooke looked at the book for about twelve seconds before beginning her test.

"Dad, what's an object pronoun?"

"Object pronoun? Let me think," I said, looking in the book because I forgot what they are. "The man gave the virus to me. Me is the object pronoun."

"Okay, got it. How about a subject pronoun?"

"He gave me the virus."

"Thanks, Dad. What about possessive pronouns?"

"The virus was his." I'm all over this.

At 4:45, my mom's caretaker Linda calls. They need food for dinner and also groceries. When there are two subjects to discuss, our words sometimes cross.

"Linda, why don't I go to Palermo's and get you and mom some nice Italian food for dinner? Want that?" I asked.

"No, she like Frosted Flakes," Linda said.

"Yes, I understand that. I was talking about dinner."

"And two onions," she said.

"I don't think you should ever eat those two together. I'll get the onions and the Frosted Flakes, but I'm trying to see what you want for dinner. Do you want Italian food?"

"Who?"

"It's a *what*, actually. Do you want spaghetti and meatballs, ravioli, or rigatoni?"

"Okay, yes."

"All right, I'll get you the spaghetti and meatballs, that sound good?"

"And two onions."

Reaalllly wants the onions.

8:30 p.m.

I am listening to the latest doctor being interviewed about the virus.

"Doctor, you are an infectious disease specialist. We are hearing that many families with the extra time on their hands are playing the old board games, like Monopoly. Is that safe?" the reporter asks.

"That actually can pose a risk," the doctor replies. "You see, every player is touching the dice first of all. And in a game like Monopoly, you have all those little plastic homes and hotels. An infected person could touch those, hand them off to another player, and that's all it may take."

I had four houses and three hotels that Mikey handed to me.

Tomorrow I need to finish my will.

APRIL 28: DAY 39

Still using the lice shampoo. Got it in my eyes this morning, so we began the day with a nice scream.

Off to Mariano's to get the onions. I walked in with the N95. I could feel people taking me in. May hang in a hardware store later.

I am in the produce section. You know those plastic bags that you tear off and put the veggies in? Apparently they have a new kind. I tear it off, but I can't open the bag. So I assume it's a bad bag and tear off another one. Cannot get it open.

I don't have nails but usually this is still pretty doable. I stand there for five full minutes. I am now watching other shoppers going through the same process. One woman with long nails and an inferior mask flicks the bag open in seconds. I'm not going near her.

Once I get it part way, I try to blow into the bag to open it. That's not happening with the N95, no sir. Have the onions and Frosted Flakes, so that's a big accomplishment for today.

3:30 p.m.

I go for a walk in the afternoon with Brooke because it is a beautiful sunny day at 70 degrees.. Rare. We are walking next to each other on the sidewalk, which is exactly where I should be with my little girl. Until she sneezes.

I used to say, "God bless you!" Now, I think, "Dr. Fauci said the droplet sprays of virus-laden respiratory tract fluid can result in aerosol transmission which could travel more than six feet outdoors depending on the wind."

I turn my head and back away from the sneeze so fast that I caught part of my neighbor's tree branch on my head and scraped my scalp. The branch is way too low over the sidewalk, so I hope the tree gets lice.

Never saw so many people out walking. Couples, parents and children, some alone with their AirPods, playing those fine f-bomb-laced tunes. It shouldn't take a worldwide pandemic for me to realize the value of a walk with my daughter.

"We finally got a nice day," I say to my neighbor Gary as we walk by his house.

"Not for long, my friend. Supposed to get a nasty storm," he says.

Forty-five minutes. In forty-five minutes the sky was that cement gray that we see in Chicago on days best described as *bleemy*. We never have "partly cloudy" here like they do in those nice climates where part of the sky is clouds, the other part blue. We get a tarp.

We walk in the house and Leona calls. Says she hopes we all got outside today because it's supposed to rain for days.

For days. That's good. It's not like we're locked in with nothing to do. I'd suggest a board game if it didn't come with a hospitalization risk.

4:30 p.m.

The girl's bathroom sink is clogged again. Illinois has its highest death toll at 144 today, so I bravely send my daughter to the store for Drano. Two large bottles. Drano.

Something happens between the moment I tell her what we need from the store and when she arrives there. She tends to come back with different items than ordered. It must come from me because Erica said I was incapable of buying the right thing from the store.

Natalie calls me from the store. "I can't find the Flume."

"Flume?" I ask.

"Yeah, I looked up and down the detergent aisle and I don't see anything called Flume."

"Probably because it hasn't been invented yet," I tell her.

"Isn't that what you asked me to get, Flume?"

"Flume? No, I didn't ask you to get Flume. I asked you to get Drano. Drano is a nice word because it sounds like drain, the thing we are trying to unclog. Flume doesn't have any of the same sounds as drain, nor any of the same letters as Drano."

"Oh, okay. I see it now."

The rain begins. The night is quiet.

Until 12:15 a.m.

The bathroom mirror is smeared with a brown color. "Brooke! What's all over the mirror and the counter?"

"I wanted to put some makeup on my dollies," she says.

"Why brown?" I ask.

"They wanted to be tan and it's never sunny here."

Can't argue with that.

APRIL 29: DAY 40

Many reflective posts on social media this morning about rain.

Rain is beauty; descending to the earth; without rain, there will be no life. The everyday showers rejoice the thirsty earth, and bless the flowering buds.

Wrong.

Not when it rains for eleven straight hours. The buds are dead. The snow killed them. And I don't think the earth is thirsty. I see large swaths of water in my backyard. It looks a lot more like a drowning.

There is a planned "parade" today to cheer and give appreciation for the teachers. I received an email that we better wear our raincoats because it's not supposed to stop.

Raincoats. I cannot imagine the look I would get from the teens if I asked them to wear a raincoat. It's hoodies and sweatshirts in layers because that makes for more laundry.

I don't think they'll be up in time for the parade anyway. At least Joey is sleeping with sufficient protein since there is a large jar of peanut butter and a spoon next to his bed.

10:23 p.m.

Blast call. Every phone in the house is ringing. It's the school. The parade is canceled. It's been rescheduled for two days from now because that's when the rain is supposed to stop—forty-one hours from now.

The parade for the teachers, that recognition is a good idea. When the stay-at-home was announced, I initially thought, "Well, this probably isn't too bad for them, they don't have to stand in class all day."

Then I tried it. Not so easy. I have a niece, Laura, who is a reading specialist. Her husband, Chris, teaches students with learning and behavioral disorders. They're not only struggling to find ways to do this through a computer; they struggle because they can't reach the students that need their help.

A friend, Missy, is a teacher. She reminded me that teachers try to identify how each student learns. It's not one-size-fits-all.

And I'm teaching my own children. In a classroom, the teachers have to deal with the bad kids, which, of course, couldn't possibly be mine.

I think I needed Erica to remind me of all this. She taught at T.F. South High School in Lansing, Illinois, with this incredible group of teachers. When you hear the backstories from them, all that goes on in a single day to educate, you realize how much they give to our children.

Erica would be saying right now, "They should have a lot more than a friggin' beep-beep parade for the teachers." You would be right, sweetheart.

3:00 p.m.

"Hey, Dad, what's a black blizzard?" Mikey asks.

"That's when you chop up Oreos in chocolate ice cream?" I answered seriously. I know my ice cream treats.

"No, this is for school, Dad. It's for history. It's not about ice cream."

Off to Google and return with "billowing clouds of black dust experienced during the Dust Bowl in the 1930s." Maybe that's what the witch was riding her bicycle through in *The Wizard of Oz*.

10:08 p.m.

It has now rained for 16 ¾ hours.

At 11:45, Brooke completes the building of a fort. I crawl in.

"Hi and welcome to my new home," she proudly says. "I have supplies for us. Pringles and hand sanitizer."

This virus has affected everything.

APRIL 30: DAY 41

I dreamt about the virus. That's sickening.

I was giving a speech at an airport—because people are always giving speeches at airports. There was a large crowd, but I discovered that none of them were there to hear me speak. They were going to a restaurant. I spotted a friend of mine in the crowd, a guy I hadn't seen for some time. He came up and gave me a big embrace and said, "How are you? How are the kids?"

I said, "Natalie has the virus."

He paused and stared at me. "Why did you let me hug you then?" He was so angry. And then, as dreams go, he turned around and flew down the terminal in his jetpack.

As if the transition was planned, Natalie comes down the stairs this morning saying, "Dad, Dad, did you see this? The Pentagon confirms that there are UFOs!"

Can't be worse than a bat.

My *Tribune* says, "The Defense Department confirmed what seekers of extraterrestrial life have long hoped to be true. They're real!"

The Pentagon released three videos of unidentified flying objects recorded by infrared camera.

Sure, why not do it now? Nothing else going on.

Can you imagine if they landed on Earth now with everyone walking around with a mask and all the hair places closed? It would be a horrible impression to leave on the rest of the solar system.

These masks are funny. I saw one guy at the gas station and either his head was inflamed or the mask was too tight because the top half of his face was so red. It looked like it might blow any second.

There is humor in almost everything if we choose to see it.

MAY 1: DAY 42

8:00 a.m.

Checking my texts and see that I received one at 2:30 a.m. from my Natalie:

"Dad, can you wake me by 2:00 so I can see the sun?" Natalie wrote. Attached is a picture of the weather forecast for today. Sunny until two.

11:00 a.m.

They're all sleeping. I hear police sirens. They seem to be getting louder. Nothing I can do. I keep working on the computer.

The sirens are getting progressively closer. Now it's cars beeping incessantly. It's on our block, in front of my house. I forgot that the teacher's parade was at 11:00 and they're driving down every block. Thirty-five cars blasting horns, three police squads with sirens on. Not one child wakes.

It's nice to see our teachers. It's nice to see the sun.

2:30 p.m.

The teacher emails to see if Brooke wants to do her Pop Bottle Project presentation on Monday. I ask Brooke how it is coming, and she snaps back, "It's not done because you never bought my Styrofoam head for Venus Williams." The things a father forgets.

I ask Natalie if she could run to the store and buy her little sister the materials. She starts leveling with Brooke about the unimportance of what material composes the head.

"Brooke, you don't need Styrofoam," she explains. "Here, use this," she says, handing her a full-sized Wiffle ball.

"I CAN'T USE THAT! IT HAS HOLES. VENUS CAN'T HAVE HOLES IN HER HEAD!"

"Brooke, I am not going to the Dollar Store and risking my life so you can have a Styrofoam head for Venus Williams!"

11:00 p.m.

We all sit down to watch a series on Netflix. It's called *Into The Night*, and is about people who get hijacked on a plane. They find out that they have to stay in darkness because if the sun comes out it will kill them.

They should have landed the plane here.

MAY 2: DAY 43

The first text of this Saturday morning is from my neighbor moT.

"We're going to war with China."

That's not good. Half the things I bought on Amazon will be delayed.

"Troops and fighter pilots are being sent to Japan. It's not for a vacation," he texts.

He gets the best intel. I don't know where that war would fit in with all the other fun we're having.

In order of importance, we have no traditional senior prom, a worldwide health pandemic with no cure, war with China, and UFOs.

What else could happen?

Brooke runs inside, "Dad, Dad, you have to come outside right now! Joey's on the roof," she says. "Something's up there!"

What does that mean, *something's up there*?

I go outside and Joe is on the roof. "What's going on?" I ask him.

"There's something in the gutters," he says. "I can hear it running back and forth."

I cannot, CANNOT have insects or rodents or raccoons in my house. I pay an exterminating company to come to the house every quarter just to keep me safe from those things.

Just as I was hoping that Joey didn't really hear anything, my neighbor Dwayne walks over.

"Hey Dave, I was going to come get you," he says. I know that the next words out of his mouth will be very bad. "I was sitting at my desk and I heard it racing in the gutter."

Racing. Which means it could catch me if I was running from it.

Joey is now squirting the hose down the gutter. I hear it. I hear the little footsteps. That sends willies up my spine.

"It got inside that area under the gutter," Dwayne says.

Did he have to say that? That means it's internal to my house structure. This is definitely worse than the war with China.

Two years ago, I saw Dwayne standing on his deck looking down at his garbage can, which was upside down. He had trapped a live animal in there and wasn't sure what to do. Given that he was standing on a deck and the can was eight feet below him, it seemed to me like he was a little apprehensive.

I told him that I heard about a time when a guy in our town had an animal trapped just like that. Eventually they moved the can. Dwayne asked, "Yeah, what happened?"

"It jumped up and killed him!"

Dwayne is enjoying a little payback today.

My neighbor behind me, Mark, hears all this. He was out planting flowers. Wonderful guy. Used to be a priest, but now has a beautiful family.

"What's going on, Dave?" Mark says. "Is there something on your roof?"

"We don't know what's up there. Think it's an animal," I tell him.

"Do you know what I found in my yard today? A snake!" Then, holding his arms out wider than his body, he says, "That sucker was this long!"

I live in a jungle. It's theoretically possible with the rain levels.

Mark isn't done. "I just held the head of the snake, picked the whole thing up, and threw it in my neighbor's yard," he says proudly. "I was going to chop its head off, and then I started feeling bad about it."

"Maybe you should have thought of it as Satan," I reply.

That yard where he threw the snake belongs to a guy who only lives in that house a few months a year and doesn't touch his property. I tell Mark that if the snake comes back to throw it in my gutter so it can eat whatever the hell is in there.

Leona calls during our animal trauma.

"I'm so bored," she says. "I've cleaned every room. I don't know when I'm gonna be able to go back to work," she says.

"I'm sure it will be soon," I offer. "You'll just have to do the ladies' hair wearing a mask."

"I can't breathe in those friggin' masks!" she says.

"You know they don't cut off the oxygen," I try to explain.

She starts crying again about Natalie, worried that they might cancel the prom. "I remember my prom," she says. "It's so much fun getting ready, taking the pictures, the flowers, you really look forward to it. The dance was shit. I didn't have any fun at the dance. But all the other stuff is good. And that's it. That's it."

I decide to do nothing about the little creature, hoping it leaves.

12:00 a.m.

We decide to watch another two episodes of *Into the Night*. The kids are snug on the couch and chairs, we have some popcorn made. I hit play and then I go to grab a glass of water.

The episode starts. I'm in the kitchen ten feet away, and I hear the noises. The "adults who aren't married having loud sex in strange positions" noises.

Where did that come from? I know where we ended the last episode. It was a bunch of people standing outside an airport at night, in another country, fueling a plane. They were all worried about the sun blazing them to death. How, how does that transition into a "loud yelling sex in strange positions" scene?

There are no words a father can use when you're thrown into that situation. What would Mr. Rogers say? *Hold on kids, sounds like an intercourse scene.* No, dads make a noise like, "ahhh woahh, yaaaa" in an effort to drown it out while you find the fast forward button. The seventeen-year-old is smirking watching me try to handle this.

Two episodes and bed. Tonight's story is about Larry Lips. He has no body. Just lips. Great at playing the horn but always needs Chapstick.

Enough activity for one day.

MAY 3 – DAY 44

Clothes on the bedroom floors. At what point do kids think, "Well, this looks like a nice open spot on the carpet, I'll leave it there for a week."

I read on Google that bending to pick up clothes on the floor "may cause the cervical disc to bulge toward the spinal canal." I can picture myself in one of those massive head braces. Try putting a mask over one of those.

2:00 p.m.

The kids went out to visit Leona this afternoon. They brought back her old bike.

"Why did you bring that back here?" I ask them. "We don't need another bike."

"Natalie wanted it," Joey answers. "It's not in bad shape. I'm just going to paint it and put some air in the tires with the compressor."

The other three make a bonfire in one of those portable fire pits you get at Home Depot. It's too heavy to move to the garage every year so it has a nice rust around the edges. Works with a camping theme.

BANG!

I run out in front because I think I know what happened. "Are you okay?" I ask Joey.

"Yeah. The front tire blew," he says. "The force actually moved that entire compressor!"

And to think Leona just bought those tires after Kennedy was elected.

Sunday evening there's an automated call from two of the three schools. "Parents, just a reminder that tomorrow, Monday, is a remote day…"

It's a good thing they called. I had no idea why the kids were home all day.

11:45 p.m.

"Dad?"

"Yes, Mikey?"

"I just thought of something," he says, smiling. "Could I transfer to a school that is already out for the year and then transfer back to mine in the fall?"

Brilliant.

MAY 4: DAY 45

The science teacher has announced that today there will be a virtual field trip to the zoo. The kids have to watch video cameras stationed by each animal at the zoo. We couldn't access the site for twenty-seven minutes because of computer issues. Brooke is now hiding in a bathroom watching TikTok while I try to figure it out.

Finally I access it.

"Brooke, come down to finish your work."

"I did it all," she yells.

"No, you didn't. Come down here."

"I finished, Dad," she says.

Now I am getting louder. "Brooke, get down here and finish your work. You're not finished!"

"Yes I a-a-am. I di-i-i-d everything," she whines.

"No you didn't! GET DOWN HERE!! YOU'RE GOING TO THE VIRTUAL ZOO RIGHT NOW!"

And based upon those words, your Honor, we believe Mr. Heilmann should be sent to an institution for a period of three years.

When I was little, if kids were disobedient, parents would threaten them with the Audy Home, the largest juvenile detention center in the world. The nuns told us that's where the homeschool kids ended up. Today, what can we say when they're locked in the house all day? Patience.

4:30 p.m.

I was driving home from the store and heard the following news announcement:

"Scientists are now confirming the presence of MURDER hornets in the state of Washington," the reporter says.

What?! Are we now in the *Twilight Zone?* I have something crawling in my gutter, snakes in the yard, and the invasion of murder hornets?

The reporter continues:

"These enormous hornets have spiked shark fins that can wipe out a honeybee hive in hours, cutting the heads off the bees and flying off with the rest of the bee's body to feed their young."

I'm sorry. That's one f---ed up hornet. THIS is what that rappers should sing about.

Of course the reporter had to bring the story home by letting us know what it can do to humans.

"..And for larger targets, the hornet's potent venom and stinger, which is long enough to puncture a beekeeping suit, are an excruciating and intolerable combination that victims liken to hot metal driving into their skin."

Maybe we should diagram the sentence so that we fully understand potent, puncture, excruciating, intolerable, and driving.

7:00 p.m.

Natalie was helping clean up after dinner and took it upon herself to vacuum the kitchen floor. That was thoughtful. Until she said, "Had they invented vacuums when you were little, Dad?"

Yes. We had vacuums. The only place that didn't was my fraternity during hell week. To clean the dirty shag carpeting we had to crawl on our knees and pick up every speck, shouting "Happy Hoover, Happy Hoooooover." That's another story.

Finally, bedtime. Brooke is brushing her teeth and I hear screams from the bathroom.

"Oh, my God, there's a bug in the sink! Natalie, kill it, I'm not going in there!"

Mikey walks into the bathroom. "Hey Brooke, it's on your iPad." (Because she can't brush her teeth without watching a YouTube video.) "It's starting to eat your iPad!"

"Mikey, noooooooooooooo!!!! You are so not funny at all."

The zoo, murder hornets, and sink bugs. Fun day.

MAY 5: DAY 46

The Interactive Science Book has the seventh-grade work for today. It's the chapter on how new species form and their rate of evolution. The very first article is entitled "Crickets, Maggots, and Flies, Oh My!"

It reminds me of my first baseball league. When I was eight, I was on the Fleas. We beat the Ants for the championship. The other teams were the Spiders, Wasps, Hornets, and Bees. I never understood why the adults were always laughing.

Back to the article:

> A male cricket chirps to attract a mate. Unfortunately, chirping attracts a parasitic fly. The female parasitic fly deposits larvae onto the cricket's back. The larvae, or maggots, burrow into the cricket and come out seven days later, killing the cricket.

I don't know of anything that is more rude than putting larvae on someone's back. But the story goes on to tell about crickets in Kauai. In the early 1990s, crickets were getting decimated by the flies. In twelve years, the cricket population returned, dominated by males who evolved into a silent population.

So when you chirp too much, it can attract annoying parasites that get under your skin. But they don't come around if you're quiet. That would be today's social media lesson.

Leona is here. First time in forty-four days. It's wonderful. She cut my hair after telling me I looked like one of those old country singers.

Maria, our cleaning lady, was supposed to come for the first time since March. She has been very helpful to us over the years.

But then she canceled.

"Can you believe that Maria? She canceled again!" Leona says. "I told her, 'Maria, that's the third time you canceled. You can't keep doing that!'"

"Why did she cancel?" I ask.

"Oh, some b.s. reason," Leona says. "She said she fell or something."

That 70-year-old woman is such a baby, not coming to clean a house after falling.

Leona cleans instead. It looks magnificent until 9:23 p.m. I walk into our family room and find nine large cups filled with a dark liquid and four hand soap dispensers where my little angel was playing with a small city of dolls.

"Hi Brookie, whatcha doing?" her magnificently calm dad asks.

"I'm playing with my dollies. They're all going to the Met Gala," she says.

Of course. Where else would they be going? "What's in all the cups?" I ask.

"They're all getting mud baths," she explains.

"I see. Do the dollies need all the hand soap that protects daddy from dying from the virus?"

"Yes, they do. After the mud bath they need soap to wash off the mud."

The grammar school announced today that from now on we will be having "restful Wednesdays." Thus begins a series of late-night Fat Tuesdays.

MAY 6: DAY 47

A call comes in on my cell phone that has the "no caller ID" flash. That's more suspect than "scam likely." I don't answer it and continue working, coughing a few times. Naturally, my first thought is that Leona infected me yesterday during the haircut.

No caller ID has left me a voicemail. It's the office of the gastroenterologist. I have a planned procedure May 12 for one of those enjoyable scopes down the throat.

But why is the doctor's office using a no caller ID? How bad is it?

"Mr Heilmann, we are planning on going forward with the procedure on the 12th, but we need you to get a COVID-19 test first. You need to call Ann at our office today.

Today. A COVID-19 test.

I call Ann and she confirms that I need to take the test. Today.

Fine, can't be difficult. I've been hearing about all the advances in the tests. The one they did on Trump was supposedly the nasal swab that is inserted up, nicks the brain, and then returns back. But from all the news reports, there are many more tests out there like saliva or maybe a blood test.

"Ann, what kind of a test will be done?" I ask.

"It's the nasal swab," she says.

"Will it hurt?" asks the grown man, father of four children.

I think she was a bit surprised. She appropriately responds, "Well, I'll give you a lollipop when I'm done if that makes it better. It's a little uncomfortable, but it's not painful," she adds.

A little uncomfortable. This is the office of the GI, the people who do the colonoscopy and tell you that the night before is a little uncomfortable. No. You drink a container of hell from the drugstore and everything you have eaten for six months exits your system. They should give the people with the virus a bottle of that stuff because I don't think anything internally could hang on given its gravitational pull.

At 3:00, I am walking out the door as I tell Joey where I'm going.

"Well, there's 1200 bucks out the door," he says. "That's what I heard the things cost."

It was nice to have the financial component introduced into the anxiety.

"I think the insurance will cover it, Joe. At least I hope so," I say.

"I heard that spike they put up your nose hits the back of your head," he wiseassingly adds. He actually used the word *spike*.

I get to the doctor's office and the nurse comes out to the car, with a nice big smile under her protective face mask and armor. The only thing I'm looking for is the length of the nasal swab. I see it and now know why there was a shortage of these nationally because the only places that had them must have been zoos.

She asks, "How are you doing today?"

"You're about to stick something up my nose that will tell me whether or not I'm going to die. I've had better moments."

And then she uses the word that no nurse should use: "Ready?"

I still had my seatbelt on just in case.

It was actually pretty mild. I was so happy to get it over with that I stopped at the butcher on my way home to increase the risk of infection.

MAY 7: DAY 48

Social studies

WRITE ABOUT IT

Write a description of Timbuktu as it was five hundred years ago. Tell about the climate and what made the community famous.

It's famous because everybody uses the phrase "from here to Timbuktu." Here's what the travel guides tell us about getting there. You start by getting multiple vaccinations, malaria tablets, and mosquito nets. Once you get there, the roads are shattered, it's mostly donkeys, and you'll only get a boat to cruise the Niger River when there's water flowing in it. That's always a plus on a boat ride.

Tell about the climate, the assignment states. It's on the southern edge of the Sahara Desert, in Mali, Africa, so we'll go with *warm*.

It used to be a very wealthy place about five hundred years ago. Had gold, trade, one hundred thousand people, and great scholars who left behind manuscripts. In fact, one sixteenth-century Timbuktu manuscript had the formula for making toothpaste. It said, take salt and sugar, mix it up with charcoal, and that "regular brushing can avoid bad breath." And, four out of five Timbuktutian dentists surveyed recommended it for their patients.

Mikey asks, "Why do we have to learn about Timbuktu five hundred years ago?"

"I don't know, Mikey. What do you think they'll be saying about us five hundred years from now?"

"They'll say I'm the oldest man alive," he says. "And probably talking about the year 2020."

If we're lucky they'll be talking about people who didn't wait for the history books and learned the lessons in real time.

Natalie:

"Do you know what I read today?"

"No, I don't," I say, expecting sarcasm.

"I learned that if you eat an orange while in the shower that it fills the shower with a citrus aroma."

"Did you try it?" I ask.

"No, I had a bowl of cream in the bath because that sounded better."

2:55 p.m.

"The U.S. is in first place with the virus," Mike says. Not the race we want to win.

8:30 p.m.

Joey tells me that he passed out last night. "It was around 5:30 in the morning," he says. "I got up to go to the bathroom and then all I remember is waking up on the floor."

"Did you feel sick? Are you feeling okay now?" Obviously, this is scary.

"Yeah, yeah. I feel fine now," he says. "It could have been the nine Dr. Peppers."

No, that couldn't be it. Everyone is supposed to have at least ten. I think I heard Dr. Fauci saying that just the other day.

"Did you drink any water yesterday?" I ask.

"No. With all the Dr. Pepper I really wasn't that thirsty."

MAY 8: DAY 49

Common Core math

Julio measured a length of yarn that was 4½ inches. How would you adjust a line plot to record the length?

You know what? I wouldn't. I would take the yarn and cut it up into little pieces and then paste it to whatever sphere we can find for Venus Williams's head on the pop bottle. Then I'd have some coffee, Julio.

My sister Cathy calls. She lives in St. Louis and was the first of the six children in our family. Her favorite phrase is "I just thought that…" which is followed by a directive. It is typically repeated two to four times in a twenty-minute conversation. It should be received as, "this is what you will do."

She calls to tell me that she ordered a gift card from Palermo's restaurant. "I just thought you could buy Mom dinner from there on Mother's Day, say around 5:00."

"Sure, I'll ask Mom on Mother's Day if that's what she has a taste for and, if so, then I'll get it," I answer.

Pause.

"Well, I just thought she'd like a nice Mother's Day dinner from there, like around 5:00," she says.

"Right. She might, but since the food will actually be going in her mouth she may have an opinion on it," I try to explain.

"I think she likes to eat around 5:00. That's what she told me. I call her every day."

"Got it."

"And I just thought Palermo's would be nice for that day."

An hour after we hung up, a card came in the mail from that same sister and my brother-in-law Bob. They know that Mother's Day is hard and sent each of the kids a little gift card and note. There is always a handwritten note, for every birthday, every holiday and every time we need a lift. My sister gets that from my mom.

As I watch Natalie open her card, we talk about how meaningful it can be when you take a few minutes to handwrite a kind note. If she remembers this, that will be a better lesson than anything on a computer screen today.

4:00 p.m.

The mayor of Chicago said today that they'll be assigning different times of the day for joggers, walkers, and bikers to use Chicago's lakefront. "It will be guided by science."

I've been working on science for four children. I haven't seen that chapter on what times joggers are most contagious when adjacent to the Great Lakes.

6:15 p.m.

"Dad?" Brooke calls. "Can you look at my hands? They're all dry and they hurt a lot."

Her little hands were red and so dry that the skin was peeling off. I felt terrible. "Oh baby, that looks really dry. Let's get some cream on those right away." I put the Eucerin cream on her that I use for dry skin, but she gives me a screaming red face.

"Does it sting?" I ask.

"A little," she quietly says. "But this should help."

Half an hour later she comes back, "Do you like how I tricked you? That was dried glue on my hands."

11:30 on this Friday night.

They're starting a *Star Wars* movie. That's fine. They can sleep late. It's thirty-eight degrees in May. Another school week down.

Until Mikey and Brooke run downstairs shouting.

"Dad, Dad!" Mikey grabs me.

"Something's in the attic. I heard it scratching!"

"I heard it too, Dad! I heard its feet and that scratching!" Brooke says, terrified.

"I'm not sleeping here tonight," Natalie says, watching the movie. "I'm not letting it eat me."

Joey comes walking up from the hole and Mikey tells him there's some animal in the attic and it's scratching.

"Let me get it," Joey says. He walks into the garage, comes back with an old pellet gun, and cocks it. "I'll kill it."

What do you know? Dwayne the Rock Johnson is here.

"What is that?" I ask him.

"It shoots little pellets. Doesn't hurt humans but it can kill that thing," he says.

"Put that down now and get it out of my house," I tell him. "You're not shooting a raccoon or whatever is up there with a pellet gun."

"Fine," he says. "Then give me a knife and I'll go up there and cut its head off."

"What? What video games are you playing?"

Googling "animals in the attic." Could be a raccoon, it says. Or a family of them. Or a rodent. Or sometimes, my article says, it's a bat.

I call the exterminator services at 12:20 a.m. I tell them it's an emergency and they agree to have someone at the house between 8:00-10:00 tomorrow.

I'm reading online about what could be up there. It says some animals can eat right through a living room ceiling.

I doubt my lymphocytes can kill whatever it is.

I'll have a little Captain Morgan now.

MAY 9: DAY 50

Didn't sleep well. Every noise, every creak was that animal on its way to my room.

The exterminator pulls in the driveway driving a small passenger car. That's not good. He needs one of those vans to carry all large equipment necessary to get this animal out of my house.

He's in his late 50s/early 60s, and his name is Jim. Throughout our conversation he refers to himself in the third person.

"So, what seems to be the problem?" Jim asks.

I tell him about what we heard in the gutters a few days ago and then the scratching last night.

"I know what's going in your head. You're thinking, 'Jim, tell me how to get rid of this thing.'"

"Yes I am, Jim."

"I'll inspect everything, but I need to tell you now that you may be looking at $1850. That's what the standard fee is if we have to send the crew out. We don't kill them, you know, with sensitivity to animals and all that. But, we lure them out. Let's take a look around the house."

We walk around and I show him where I heard this thing in the gutter.

"I don't see where an animal would get in. Everything is sealed and in good shape."

We had a new roof and gutters put on last summer. Maybe we sealed it inside for a year and it grew.

Jim is standing in the backyard looking at the house. "Now you're probably thinking, 'Jim, if everything is sealed, what can you guys do?' And I will then tell you all about the $1850. The problem is that this cost covers sealing up holes, usually for people who let their homes fall apart," he says.

"Do you want to check out the attic?" I ask.

"That's the scary part, but let's do it," Jim says.

He is on the second floor and I remain on the first in case it leaps at his neck.

After fifteen minutes up there, he comes back down. "Well, I don't see any poop or tracks. As I see it, you've got three choices. The first is you just hope it goes away. Now, I can tell by the look on your face that your stress level is at six right now and headed to seven, so you probably don't want option one."

"No, Jim, I don't. What's the second?"

"One thousand eight hundred fifty dollars. We send out a manager and he'll try to lure it out. Can't kill it because we don't want to be on social media saying we're animal killers. We have this device that will lure them out, and once they're out, they can't get back in. We have that in your yard. Once it captures them and closes, have to warn you it'll be screaming pretty loud. Sometimes their paws are bleeding because they've been trying to scratch out of the trap for hours before we can get there to pick up the cage. Try to ignore it."

"Oh, my God."

"Here's the other problem," he adds. "We may lure out the mother, but if it has babies up there, then the babies are going to start screaming every night because their mother isn't there. And we've got to go back and try to get them."

"This keeps getting better, Jim."

"Now, the third option is calling a trapper. They are about eight hundred bucks. What they'll do is trap the mother, and then if there are babies, they'll bring the animal back up into your house so that the babies will get with the mother and then they'll take them all out of there."

That's thoughtful. I ask him if they have a trapper. "If we call the trapper, then it's a thousand dollars. We have to cover insurance and all that," he says.

He continues, "You're saying, 'Jim, I've never called a trapper.' Let me tell you something. These guys have the long hair down their backs, they smoke, and have snakes painted all over the sides of their vans. Lot of tattoos. They do their thing and then they get drunk and party; so I tell people, you know, you might want to call and make sure they come in the morning. I told one customer, 'Lady, don't be offering him any beer because he'll stay all day.'"

Jim is not done.

"I know you're sitting there at a stress level of seven," he continues, "and you're saying to yourself, 'Jim, could this be any worse?' Well, I'm gonna bring your stress level above a nine right now."

That's nice.

"Some of these animals eat your electrical. Then they start pooping and urinating all over the attic."

Yes, I would think that the electrical might go through the system quickly. Their own little version of the night before a colonoscopy.

"Then they have babies and they're running all over the place up there. All of it can be unsafe to humans."

Ya think?

"So what we have to do is remove everything, tear out the insulation, sanitize the entire attic, and put in new insulation. You're looking at $7000."

"I am at the nine now, Jim."

"Sometimes people hear those noises and don't do anything about it. Had a lady one time who let it go for months. When I got there, poop all over the place. The old woman told me that she just started hearing the noises and I said, 'Ma'am, it's time to tell Jim the truth.'"

"What do you think I should do, Jim?".

"Well, I'm not allowed to make recommendations other than our company," he says, glancing around. "Now, if we were in a bar what would I tell you? Are we in a bar right now Dave, can we talk?"

"Yes, we are in a bar, Jim. I may go to a bar soon."

"Call the trapper," Jim says.

Then he tells me that he also is working a second job, night shift, at a factory that supplies food. He takes temperatures of employees to make sure everyone is safe.

"I guess I'm a first responder at heart."

I hope we all are in some way.

I have messages out to several trappers. A guy calls me from Indiana, only about forty minutes from where we live. He says, "No, we're not going into Illinois these days given the state of the virus there." Thank you for that.

A woman named Louise calls. Hoarse, husky voice. Probably smoked for forty years. I'm judging her seven seconds into the call. She says it's $265 to set the trap and then another $75 to remove the animal. So, there are people who don't spend the $75 and leave the animal up there?

The trapper came by at 3:00. Clean-cut, professional. Checked everything for ninety minutes. No raccoons, no big rodents. May have had a mouse and he threw pellets down that will take care of it.

We talk about everything people are going through with the coronavirus. He has kids.

"Dave, I tell them, don't be so upset about staying inside. You're so lucky with what you have these days. Be grateful. There are things I have to give up too. I'd love to be camping."

Camping. What do you know.

MAY 10: DAY 51

The high is 40.5 degrees today. I look at the weather section in the paper to see if the week will get any better.

The headline of the weather section reads, "What happened to spring? Call it Schafskälte!" This is a German word for cold sheep because right after they shear the wool off the sheep, this nasty cold whips in around June. That's what it feels like here.

Schafskälte may be second only to schadenfreude, which is taking pleasure in the pain of other people. Like my friends who text me from Florida and say, "So how's it going?"

Today's adventure will be a trip to Home Depot because I have to return an item. I am incapable of purchasing the right product the first time at that store.

There is one person in front of me at the customer return desk. I believe this young woman is either performing surgery this afternoon or is very meticulous about protecting herself from the virus. She has on two pairs of gloves—two—and hands the returns guy her driver's license. He hands it back five seconds later, and she holds it up in the air in front of his face, as if she can see the virus attached to it, and wipes clean every edge of the license.

She was returning eight items. After eleven minutes, I faced away from her and quietly coughed into my mask. This seemed to accelerate things.

I remember while I was there that my trapper said I need caulk. I ask a guy where it is and head to that aisle. I turn down what apparently is the drill lane, and there is a big guy: a customer, no mask. I pass him and see two other guys, no masks. I guess if they get the virus they'll just beat its ass.

I finally arrive at the caulk aisle and see what I think is the product. But these tubes say sealant and silicone, not caulk. The man who works there is now passing behind me and says, "Finding what you need, sir?"

I cannot bring myself to ask, "Is this caulk?" When you're standing there with an N95, you have to know caulk. And Allen wrenches. Disguising my ignorance I ask, "Is this all the caulk you guys have?" This implies that I, being a caulk expert, don't see the kind I normally use.

"Yes, sir. That's all the caulk we have."

Bingo. I buy two tubes.

Joey walks in an hour later and spots the caulk in the garage. Any time I buy anything from that store and put it by the toolbox, he lectures me on my errors.

"Did you get a caulk gun?" he asks.

"Can't you just squeeze it, like toothpaste?" I ask. It's probably what the Timbuktutians did.

"No, Dad," he sighs, walking away.

Today is Mother's Day. Children need their mom. I learn that over and over, every single day. I'm lucky to have mine.

I miss my sweetheart so much.

MAY 11: DAY 52

Headline of a *Tribune* editorial this Monday morning:

"Sorry, Illinois. Florida is doing this whole reopening thing right."

We covered this yesterday, didn't we? People who take pleasure in others' pain?

The article is from a former *Tribune* columnist who has moved to Florida. He says that the Illinois polls "treat people like sheep." Coldly, without the wool, I'm sure. He feels compelled to add that under the abundant Florida sunshine, he and his wife enjoyed the ocean views while splitting a "fresh-baked peanut butter Pizooke topped with rich vanilla bean ice cream." I believe the word is schadenfreude, yes?

Today is a big day. It's the Zoom presentation of Venus Williams as a pop bottle and Natalie's AP US Government and Politics test.

I'm trying to help Natalie prepare. There are about 655,000 articles and videos on taking AP exams, which makes me wonder why we don't AP everything for college and save the $200,000.

And men, I hate to say this, but up to this point in our nation's history, our gender has made most of the mistakes. There was one awful woman I found named Delphine LaLaurie, who was vicious to slaves. That's some name, Delphine. I picture a brooding aristocrat with six feet of mean black hair. Maybe a bad mole.

The AP test, because it is online, has been reduced to a forty-minute exam where you play "beat the clock" with hard questions. The time limits for exams like this—the ACT, and many others—puzzle me. I understand if you're in a flight simulator learning how to land a plane without crashing that this might require a quick response, but we're talking about US history here. They're all dead.

11:30 a.m.

Third-grade English

> Read the following story about Randall and his pet and create a title for the narrative.
>
> What a horrible morning. My pet snake Snerdly was missing. Where could he be? First I looked in the living room. I checked under the couch cushions. I thought I heard soft shooshing sounds, but I couldn't find my snake. Then I looked in the closet. I saw something long and slithery behind the coats. Was it Snerdly? No, it was ribbon. Then I went to the laundry room. There was Snerdly, fast asleep on top of the dryer! I was never so happy to see him.
>
> Use the information in the story to create a title for the narrative.

Randall has a pet snake that is sitting on a dryer? Who are these people? Don't any of these characters in the education books ever have a dog?

Answer: The Trapper's Son

1:00 p.m.

I get an email reminder from Joey's teacher that his science project is due Wednesday. Today is Monday.

"Joey, wake up. Do you have a science project due?"

"What?" I get the "Who the hell are you?" look I get every day when I wake him up.

"Wake up. What is your science project?"

"We have to design an invention to fix a problem."

Well, that's specific. "How about a vaccine?" I suggest.

"Dad. Please."

"So the assignment is to pick anything, any problem, and come up with an invention or plan that would take care of it?"

"Yeah. That's it, Dad."

"What problem did you pick?"

"How to get all the peanut butter out of a jar."

Well, that's one that keeps me up nights. "Really, Joe? That's really what you picked?"

"The teacher approved it."

I assume he likes peanut butter. "Have you designed this thing yet?"

"No, it's only Monday. It's not due until Wednesday."

"How long did you have to do it?"

"About two months."

Now you get to do the whole thing in two days. Good practice for the AP tests.

2:00 p.m.

The pop bottle presentation begins. One of Venus's arms, which are toothpicks, falls off. This is now a presentation of a one-armed, Styrofoam-headed tennis professional. I was proud to hear my little girl say why she picked Venus: Because she overcame racism as a child and served as a role model for African-American girls all over the world, of what they can accomplish.

What a lesson from a little pop bottle.

MAY 12: DAY 53

The freshman social studies work for today presents this to resolve:

How did Justinian's Code have an impact beyond the Byzantine Empire?

Its biggest impact was the seizure it caused a father to have 1459 years later, trying to figure out who Justinian was and why he gets to have a code. Joe is too tired to answer after defeating the Minecraft Ender Dragon last night.

We are referring to the Eastern Roman Empire that got its name from a city called Byzantium. Sounds like a place with great fireworks. Anyhow, for the geography-starved, this eventually became Constantinople and then in 1930 Istanbul. The various emperors and lord high rulers have changed the name over the years so that we keep talking about them.

Justinian had some bad politicians before him, if you can believe that. So he had a team of lawyers go through all the laws and ordinances of the empires, weed out the junk and corrupt laws, and compile one uniform set that was designed to apply to everyone. It's actually the basis for modern civil law in Europe today. One good one was, "Proof lies on him who asserts, not on him who denies." We call that innocent until proven guilty.

At 11:45 the Blue Angels do a flyover. Maybe they can find the UFOs.

After a quick endoscopy, I head to Mariano's to get dinner. I'm walking by the pickles, a good eight feet away from anybody, and a woman is approaching from the opposite direction, hugging the refrigeration rail. Just when we're passing each other, she turns and barks out this cough laterally at me. Extremely dry cough, like a hacking animal. I know she's got it. The only saving grace is that there was a guy trying to make a move around me and I think he may have intercepted the infection. That's what you get for violating the zone.

I need two sweet potatoes and some chicken breasts to bring to my mom. There's a woman wearing black gloves who is standing in front of the sweet potatoes. I have a grocery store pandemic move that I've learned, where I walk somewhat close to a person with my cart, then take three big steps back. They usually notice, feel guilty that they're blocking me, apologize, and vacate.

I try it and it doesn't work. I watch her pick up and feel thirteen different potatoes. She puts two in her plastic bag. She doesn't realize, but the side of the plastic bag is completely torn open because of the sharp edge of the potatoes. Rookie mistake. Sweet potatoes get double-bagged.

I should have told her, but I didn't. I wanted to see them fall on the floor.

She starts walking away and as I move into position, I hear thud, thud. "Oh no!" I can see her inching back toward the stand to get two new ones, so I took a few seconds longer to make my choices.

3:00 p.m.

Governor Pritzker says that the peak, which was thought to be hitting in April, then May, now may be June. The news just for today, in Illinois:

- Over 4,000 more coronavirus cases
- 144 Deaths
- New York reports that COVID-19 may lead to Kawasaki Syndrome in children, which can be fatal
- Report out that structural racism is leading to higher death rate
- Dr. Fauci tells the Senate that reopening too quickly will mean more deaths
- Churches are threatening lawsuits
- The Mayor warns that sports may not return by July
- The Governor says the State needs millions to fund basic services
- Restaurants are going out of business every day.

In one 24-hour news cycle, we receive more bad news than we're used to receiving over months. And it repeats, every day. And it comes at a time when what we turn to for a release—parties, entertainment, arts, sports—are all shut down. We have no control over it.

That's a lot of stress. Some people say this may be one of the all-time worst years in history. If it is we should at least have shirts made or something.

Here's a thought. The Mayo Clinic now tells us that humor stimulates heart muscles, lowers blood pressure, and improves the immune system. Oxford tells us that laughter releases endorphins in the brain, which reduces stress and lifts us emotionally.

That is science we can follow every day.

MAY 13: DAY 54

The third-grade social studies jump from a chapter titled "The Railroad Cars Are Coming!" to "Opportunity Cost." That's a natural progression, choo-choos to Econ 101.

Brooke shouts from the other room, "Dad, is the most important column for a budget the length of a bat?"

The thoughts that go through my head.

"I'm not sure what you mean," I say in the always pleasant tone. I go and look at the book, and I see that the example of a budget is a young girl who wants to save up enough money to buy a baseball bat.

"Oh that kind of bat," I say. "No, that was the example they used in the book. The most important column for a budget is Amazon Prime expenses."

12:15 p.m.

The grammar school English book is called *Voyages in English: Grammar and Writing.*

I'd rather be one on one of those cruise ships with the virus than on a grammar voyage.

The assignment:

"Imagine that you are giving a surprise party for your friend. Write five sentences detailing the planning procedure and use two intensive and two reflexive pronouns in your writing."

Or we send out an Evite in eleven seconds. Then again, it may not matter because half the people don't understand what RSVP means. It's French—répondez s'il vous plaît—and it means please respond BY THE DATE I REQUEST SO THAT I KNOW HOW MUCH FOOD TO ORDER AND DON'T ASK THE DAY BEFORE CAN BILLY STILL COME, I FORGOT TO SEND BACK MY RESPONSE!

Answer:

Dave, himself, planned a birthday party for ten children at the overpriced jumpy-jump place. (Intensive)

After screaming at moms for not sending an RSVP, he earned himself a reputation as a curmudgeon. (Reflexive)

MAY 14: DAY 55

Today was the last day of high school for my Natalie.

She didn't complain, but my heart breaks that my little girl didn't get the last two months of her senior year of high school, which can be filled with precious memories. Then again, half the people that I went to prom with ended the night in wicked fights with their girlfriends.

It dawned on me this fifty-fifth day of lockdown, as I thought about her last day of high school, that this begins the last three months I have her at home before college. The thoughts that go through a parent's head.

My first is that she has already lost so much without her mom. It seems like Erica and I just brought her home from the hospital, wondering if she'd ever stop crying at night. Ever. Then you blink and she's off to college.

And then after that, life. Whatever it holds.

I told her that she could forever tell her kids, "I don't want to hear about how rough it is. I was in the COVID class."

Then again, there were those who left high school and were told they were going to Vietnam, and before that other wars.

And all those children alive in the roaring twenties, who suddenly were greeted with 1929 and a life of bare minimums during the Great Depression.

The life-altering tremors have hit many in our nation's short history. You just never want it to happen to your child.

The irony is that the crisis that has caused the greatest challenges to learning is simultaneously giving us so much to learn from: health, education, science, human relationships, finance. We may never live through a time of so many teachable moments.

What can the seniors heading off to college learn now? It's not "what you major in." Look at the passionate and selfless doctors and nurses who walk into hospitals every day, not knowing if they will walk out with a life-threatening illness that could seriously harm their own family. It reminds me of the firemen or police officers who ran into the World Trade Center when everyone else was running out.

It's not the field you choose, or the money you make, seniors. It's having the character to give more of yourself than you know you even have at the exact time when others need you the most.

That changes the world.

Days when your child finishes their last day of high school make you more reflective.

MAY 15: DAY 56

"It's the new normal."

I've heard this now…mmmm… fifty billion times? It's causing ear burn. Are we out of words that we can't find other phrases? There are so many words to choose from. That's the cool thing about talking. You mix them up, different meanings, lots of syllables. It can be a hoot.

Besides, I don't know that we're using the right phrase. "Normal" is when things are not different or batshit crazy. For example, when a person drives through a bakery store window, we might say he wasn't acting normally. Or the Great Depression, that's not normal. I doubt my grandmother said to my grandfather when he was out of work, "Well, Oscar, it's just the new normal."

The truth is that there is nothing remotely normal about any of this. It came out of nowhere. No one knows how to solve it. The older you are, the scarier it gets. It's the Common Core virus. That cannot be allowed as the new normal.

I heard the magic words again this morning when the very chipper store clerk, with green and blue streaked hair, was taking in a complaint about the new one-way aisles in the grocery store. "It's the new normal!" she chirped.

Why, why do we need one-way aisles? We aren't trained to look at the floors to follow arrows on them. We look up, to the side, in freezers. We don't look down. I saw one poor man who looked like he hit one of those electric fences for dogs. I heard "OH, SHIT!" and he whipped the cart in reverse like he'd been tasered.

Did someone do a study on the infection rate of people coming down the aisle from the other direction? Is there science on this, or is it the science of "follow along, the other store did it." A person going the same way you are, in front of you, who sneezes on the Doritos, which you then grab, is harmless. But that clown coming the other way has to be stopped.

My biggest problem is that if I have to walk all the way around the aisle the opposite way, I'll forget what I was looking for.

Evening.

I see a light on in the basement. It's a lamp in that closet (now technology fortress) that Joey has built. Have to step on the beanbag bed to reach the lamp. Out of the corner of my eye I see something move…just a tiny bit. Look down and, in a small plastic Tupperware is a one-inch turtle.

"Joey!"

"Yeah?"

"Why is there a turtle in the closet?" I ask for the first time in my life.

"Oh, that's Sheldon. I found him. He won't bite."

I am so tired of little crawly things.

MAY 16: DAY 57

Was it necessary for people to hoard cleaning supplies? Really? I understand the hand soap and the toilet paper. But do they have to take all the cleaning solutions too?

The grocery stores were out so the kids went to the Dollar Store. They bought this product called "LA Totally Awesome Cleaner." Under that splashy title it says, "With Bleach!"

I haven't used this product before. I don't know what the significance of "LA" is in the title. Maybe it's what the stars use. I'd be more persuaded by an "NY" after hearing the Governor Cuomo telethon for two months. He's always saying, "New Yorkers are tough!" I think if I saw "NY Tough" on some cleaning product, I'd rationalize, "Well, they have all those rats, they're tough; this would probably work on my sink." I wouldn't feel the same way about "Paris Away," although I expect it would smell nice.

Anyhow, I have no choice but to use the bottle of Totally Awesome. It should be superior to Fantastik, my normal product, because the synonyms for awesome are "breathtaking" and "astonishing," whereas Fantastik is merely "great" or "impressive." Logically, I have the superior product.

I would prefer a product called "This Shit Is The BOMB!"

1:12 p.m.

Graduation parade beeps for our friend down the street who is graduating from high school. Mikey's birthday is coming up, but his friends are too young to drive by for a birthday parade. They're going to ride bikes by and scream.

4:30 p.m.

I walk in the house with Joey. He looks at the kitchen table and says, "Sheldon's gone!"

"Why was he on our kitchen table?" I ask.

"Joey, you stuck him in a plastic bin with a sponge," his little sister lectures. "You could have killed it."

"I did exactly what the website said to do," Joey argues. "I put a little bit of lettuce in there with a wet sponge."

I don't know why we're responsible for making this thing bigger. I let them know that I wanted the turtle outside and so that's where it is.

"Dad, if it rains, can we put him in the garage?" Mikey asks. Mikey is nice to everything.

"Turtles live outside and they can swim, Mikey," says the father with expertise in reptile care. "Where are the turtle's parents anyway?" I want to know. I don't want some angry turtle parents chewing my Amazon boxes.

"Turtles have their babies and leave them to figure everything out for themselves, Dad," Joey educates me.

There's a thought.

Sheldon is in the yard. For now. Supposed to rain for nine hours tomorrow because we had twenty-six minutes of sun today.

MAY 17: DAY 58

Front page of the *Tribune*:

"Weeks of clear skies over Los Angeles, New Delhi, Wuhan, and other soot-choked cities are signs of how the coronavirus lockdown has improved air quality around the planet...But for reasons that have yet to be fully explained, not in Chicago and the suburbs..."

That's the top story in Chicagoland this Sunday morning. It's nice to live in the county that is leading the nation in virus and soot. Maybe LA is cleaner because everyone is using Totally Awesome.

Turn the page to the Weather headline.

"Above Normal May Rainfall On The Rise." The year 2020 is on pace to be the "wettest May in the 150 years of Chicago precipitation records." That takes us back to Lincoln. That's nice.

But let's look for positives. As I scroll the news pages, it is nice to see the number of companies with warm messages to readers, letting people know that they are there to help.

Like this one.

"We have your back. We are all in this together."

"Stop in today and lease a Cadillac Escalade for $839/month."

That is so thoughtful. Here I am lying awake at night wondering "what would make the drive-by beep-beep parades better for humanity?" and bingo, these guys have my back. I'd be there this afternoon if there wasn't a hurricane.

2:00 p.m.

There is now a small Barbie Doll umbrella that Brooke has placed over the flowerpot of dirt where Sheldon is living.

8:00 p.m.

I get an email from Mikey's teacher. He's missing seven assignments and needs to submit them "or he'll get an 'incomplete' for a grade."

And it's social studies. Google Classroom, Chapter 10.

1. Who is Miguel Hidalgo and what did he accomplish?

No idea. Google search, find his name: Don Miguel Gregorio Antonio Francisco Ignacio Hidalgo-Costilla y Gallaga Mandarte Villaseñor.

But his friends called him Bucky.

I open the article, twenty paragraphs. Okay, we're not reading that. Back to the lesson. Now I have to find in what chapter they talked about this man, who I'm not happy with right now.

As I'm looking, Joe calls up from downstairs.

"Dad, you might want to see this."

Not those words. Anything but those words. Something is broken or ruined, or there's some dead animal.

"What is it, Joe?"

"There's water all over the basement."

Of course there is. Because we now live in a jungle. After an hour of cleanup, Joe asks whether they can walk over to a nearby wetlands to see how flooded it is. May as well. No one's out.

"Hey, Dad, can I go, too?" Mikey asks.

"I thought we were doing this test together."

"I won't be long. You can keep working on it though, if you want," he says with way too big of a smirk.

Fine. They go. I can help him a little.

Found Hidalgo. He was a Mexican priest who organized an army and freed several provinces from Spanish rule before he was executed in 1811.

Interesting, a priest. So it was *Father* Don Miguel Gregorio Antonio Francisco Ignacio Hidalgo-Costilla y Gallaga Mandarte Villaseñor. I can only imagine the conversation when he met Saint Peter at the pearly gates.

"Okay, name?"

"Yes, hello, Saint Peter. My name is Don Miguel."

"Okay, Don Miguel, thank you," Peter replies.

"No, no, no, I'm not finished. It's Don Miguel Gregorio Antonio, Francisco, Ignacio Hidal—"

"Great. Excuse me. Linus, you want to handle this one?"

10:00 p.m.

The kids get back home.

"The water was about five feet deep over there," Joey reports.

"Please tell me you guys didn't go in that water," says the clean dad.

"Just up to our waists," Joey says proudly. "And guess what? I killed a snake with my boot!"

MAY 18: DAY 59

Brooke has a test on ecosystems. Here is question 7:

> 7. Desert snakes eat kangaroo rats. What do you think would happen to the population of rats if the population of desert snakes grows larger?

A kangaroo rat? Really? Does it jump? I don't think nine-year-olds should be exposed to kangaroo rats because it could affect their father's sleep. As soon as they announced e-learning, that question should have been banned. I can't answer it. All I'm thinking about is this giant colony of rats jumping through the desert.

Dad's answer: I really don't care what happens to those populations as long as they are a million miles from me.

1:30 p.m.

"Dad, you wanna come out here?" Joe calls.

This comes after less than twelve hours from the, "Dad, you need to see this" line last night. He's outside so I'm not sure how bad anything could be.

"What is it, Joe?" I ask, hoping for some kind of a benign response.

"There's eggs on the side of the house."

Someone egged our house? In the middle of a pandemic, kids actually egged our house?

"No… something laid eggs by the side of our house."

Well, I know it's not a chicken. Creatures in the attic, snakes in the yard, a turtle on the deck, hornets on the way, eggs on the side of the house. Welcome to Dave's ecosystem.

I walk over to the side of the house and Joe points them out under a pile of leaves that gathered over the winter. "Whatever it is has been laying eggs and leaving them under those leaves, Dad. I think there's a lot of them."

Of course there are. Of course there are a lot of them. It's easier for a dozen of them to kill me than just one.

I decide to socially distance from them and tell Joey to grab a shovel and place the eggs into a container.

"There are at least fifteen, Dad," Joe says. "What do you think they are?"

"Probably kangaroo rats, with my luck," I tell him. "Take them to wherever you killed the snake last night."

MAY 19: DAY 60

Finally, a headline that does not talk about the virus.

"RAIN OVERWHELMS REGION"

Do you know what the third-grade assignment is today? The weather. The question on page 257 of the Pearson Realize book is:

3. LIST THE STEPS OF THE WATER CYCLE

Answer:

1. It starts in my basement
2. Travels through 26 wet towels into my washing machine
3. Washing machine empties into sewer, water gets dirtied, then drains in lake
4. Dirty water is absorbed and forms large stationary cloud over home for 1-7 months
5. Rains on my house, creating climate for animals

My little sister Suzy calls me this Tuesday morning. She's the quietest in the family because the rest of us used up all the airtime. Warm, kind, and believes that everyone should be limited to about twenty words a day. She works in an office at the Board of Trade building. No one is there and she likes it that way. No words.

"Dave, everyone riding the elevators here now has to face the wall," she says. "At first I thought it was stupid, but then a guy gets on with a really big chin. Looked like he could fight a pelican for a carp. The new rule kept him quiet for twenty floors, so I'm good with it now."

I tell her about the mice in the attic. She says, "I had one in my washer. It was running around and around like it was a circus, so I ran out of the house."

She wins.

It's probably good to remember that no matter how bad things seem, someone likely has it worse. My niece Lisa has six little kids and had to evacuate a house because of rats. Then run from wildfires.

Our family is scarred by these things because when I was eight years old, we had rats in our landscaping stones. It was a decent neighborhood, but the rats found us. The police set this big trap. One morning my mom walked out the back door, and when she came back toward the front, she saw the lightweight rocking chair on the front porch moving. The rat escaped from the trap and was on the base of the chair, rocking it.

We called the police because they had one officer in charge of this back then. By the time he arrived the rat was crawling up the front door, bleeding. He killed it with a nightstick.

At that time there was a small community newspaper. Front page the following week: "Rat Crawls Up Resident's Front Door!"

My friends didn't play at our house for a while.

MAY 20: DAY 61

Maria is coming today to clean the house. She likes to yell at me about things that jam the vacuum since she's gone through five. What makes their way to the floor of the bathroom every day are these little circular rubber bands my daughters use to do something with their hair. They are smaller than a dime and come in plastic packages containing 1.5 million of them. It's good that I search the floor for these because that's when I find the daily wear contact lenses that miss the garbage can and harden on the floor.

Maria brought a second woman with her today, Helen. First thing she tells me is that Helen's friend was cleaning a house in a different suburb, and when she walked out of the house the police gave the woman a $500 ticket for working there. Maria says, "But the lady who owned the house took the ticket and said she'd pay it."

I assured her that we would do the exact same thing if she got a ticket. She can take it to that lady's house and have her pay it.

12:00 p.m.

I talk to principal Margo today and tell her that I heard a rumor that school may end May 27 instead of June 5.

"No, we aren't doing that," she tells me. "I'd like to end early because the state would allow it, and I know it's been hard for the kids and the teachers, but the Archdiocese and Catholic Schools said no. We have to go to the last day."

Yes, because if we ended earlier there wouldn't be as much suffering.

2:00 p.m.

While we don't know if colleges will be starting up in the fall, we're still hoping. Natalie is working on picking the classes she'll take. She is most concerned about taking Spanish, which is a struggle. I tell her to check any student reviews on her college professors because a great teacher makes all the difference.

"There's only one instructor for the class I have to take," she says.

She finds the reviews on this professor. Ranks a 1 on a 5 scale, with 5 being the highest.

"It says that she's rude, condescending, races through material, gives homework every night to keep you busy, and is a hard grader."

Maybe that was one frustrated student.

"Here's another one," she says. "TERRIBLE! DON'T TAKE THIS CLASS. You'd be better off starting over with a new language for three semesters."

And then this subtle review: "This professor is mean!" Mean?

4:30 p.m.

News is coming out about a northern Illinois suburb which has the largest number of coronavirus deaths. The article included a note that the suburb with the second highest number of deaths is where I live. It didn't mention who was third, only the gold and silver medal winners. Out of 135 suburbs in Cook County, Number 2 in deaths is right here.

MAY 21: DAY 62

Take my car to the muffler place. I assume because of my N95, the manager thinks I know about cars. He says, "I just had a guy in here who has a Ford GT Turbo. That beast has carbon fiber wheels. Do you know what the lug nuts weigh?" he asks.

"No. Actually I don't. I don't know what any lug nuts weigh."

"They're lighter than a nickel," he says.

How about that? They should add that to the science quizzes.

More social studies today.

Why do you think farming did not develop extensively in arctic and subarctic regions in 1600?

Because I've never had corn from the North Pole.

11:00 p.m.

It is a nice night and the neighbors are sitting out. Jordan and Brad next door, with moT and Maura. I walk by to see how everyone is doing. Maura tells me that she's afraid moT is going to have a heart attack because they bought a pool last year and now ducks are landing in it and playing all day. moT bought a giant porcelain owl to put in his yard because he was told this is the equivalent of a scarecrow for ducks.

The next day the ducks were mating on the owl.

Brad asks how my kids are doing. He's always there to help. I tell them we're getting along. Natalie sometimes goes for drives just to get out of the house. She's always been careful, no accidents or tickets.

It was good to get out.

MAY 22: DAY 63

AT&T calls, warning me that I haven't paid my landline bill. I tell them that everyone in my house has the virus, but I can get that check in an envelope, which I would lick and seal and get to their office right away.

"No rush, take your time," he says.

12:45 p.m.

Oxford, the university, not the comma, announces that they are beginning Phase II of clinical trials on a potential coronavirus vaccine. I'm optimistic. I do believe that when the greatest minds from all over the world are working on solving the same problem, they'll find an answer.

It wasn't like that in 1918 during the Spanish flu. More than fifty million people died. The average life expectancy in America dropped by twelve years in 1918.

They didn't find a vaccine. People either died or developed immunity. I'm thankful that a century of teachers have molded these smart people who will come up with a cure and save lives.

3:14 p.m.

Natalie calls. "Dad, I was in a car accident," she says.

This would be sixteen hours and forty-four minutes after telling my neighbors how fortunate we were that she hadn't been in an accident or received any tickets. I knew it! I knew as I was saying that last night that I should have kept my mouth shut.

She wasn't hurt, and neither was Brooke, who was with her. I ask them where they are.

"We went to a Krispy Kreme in Chicago because I heard that their coffee is good."

There's an essential need.

I go to the accident site and see the nice smashed cars. I ask Brooke if she is okay.

"Natalie thinks that paramedic over there is pretty hot," said the nine-year-old.

Within an hour, after the police left and they made their undeterred Krispy Kreme stop, they are home. I ask Natalie how she is doing.

"Look at this," she said pointing to the drink from Krispy Kreme. "They call this a medium? Look how small it is. That's ridiculous." She's back to normal.

"OH NO, SHELDON'S GONE! HE'S NOT IN HIS HOME!!" Brooke screams.

I look in the little plastic container and he's gone. The one-inch turtle could not have climbed out of that container. I started thinking that some bird swooped down for a crunchy treat but I can't say that to her.

She starts sobbing about Sheldon. What words can I come up with to make everything better?

"Maybe he wanted to go off and die somewhere."

"DAD!!"

Okay, not those words.

Natalie calls Joey. "Joey, do you know where Sheldon is?"

"Yeah, I've got him with me," Joeys says. "I decided to take him on his first bike ride."

"What's wrong with you, Joey?" Brooke says. "You can't take turtles on a bike ride! You are SO MEAN!"

Meanwhile, the religion test was due at five o'clock. Missed that one. I told Mikey to write down that we're doing it on God's time, which is far longer.

MAY 23: DAY 64

Sheldon is dead. He survived the bike ride but something happened overnight.

I ask Brooke if she is sure, and she holds him up to my face and says, "Look, he's stiff and his arms and legs are sticking out."

Her little heart is broken. "I should have done more with him," she cries.

I try to console her. Her comforting older sister says, "Maybe he died because he hated his name so much." Her nickname should be "Ice."

"I think when turtles die you wear bright colors instead of black," Nat piles on.

They decide to go to the cemetery to bury him. It had been a sunny morning outside, but was getting cloudy. Not one minute after they leave, a bulletin comes over the internet news.

Effective: 2020-05-23 15:02:00 CDT Tornado Warning!

> Urgency: Immediate Severity: Extreme Certainty: TAKE COVER NOW! Move to a basement or an interior room on the lowest floor of a sturdy building. HAZARD...Tornado and hail up to two inches in diameter. IMPACT...Flying debris will be dangerous!

And social distancing has now been increased to thirty miles.

The funeral is rescheduled to tomorrow because of storms. The turtle gods are crying.

4:30 p.m.

Mikey has Spanish work that needs to be turned in. It's a day late. I took Spanish in high school and college and can't remember a thing. I believe that por que means both why and because, which must be fun during arguments with a child.

I am going to review Mikey's work, and if it's close, we're done. The assignment lists various hobbies a person might have and they have to write about it. One is "Collecting Rocks."

The worksheet states:

> Por que alguin querria recoger rocas? (Why would someone want to collect rocks?)

Mikey's response:

> Honestly, what in the world would someone be thinking if they collected rocks? Rocks are an absolutely terrible thing to collect.

Not sure where he gets that attitude.

8:00 p.m.

I read that this Saturday Shakespeare's Globe Theatre in London may permanently close.

Tough to read that. It's Erica's birthday.

There were a lot of tears today.

MAY 24: DAY 65

Most of us take eight years of addition, subtraction, multiplication, division in grammar school; four years of algebra, calculus, trigonometry, geometry in high school; and possibly additional years of math in college. Yet, we have to be shown, with tape, everywhere, what six feet is. Every floor of every store.

I went to buy plants and flowers for our house.

The store had an aisle roped off outside so that people remained in single file. Every six feet they had a sign that said STOP HERE! CUSTOMERS MUST REMAIN 6 FEET APART! There were fifteen signs in a row in case you lost your mind in the prior six feet of travel.

11:00 a.m.

Sheldon's funeral. Brooke asked us all if we would wear black and we did. Joey gives the eulogy and talks about Sheldon's last bike ride. We didn't want to laugh in front of Brooke, so we tried to keep it together.

I didn't know that she had also written a brief speech:

> Since Joey brought you home and put you on a sponge, I knew I wanted to take care of feeding you, training you, and to take care of you. I know I am not a turtle but I think I am a pretty good mom. I know you are up in heaven with mom, grandpa and uncle Joe. I miss you. I love you. I hope you had a nice life.
>
> Love, Brooke

The beauty of a child's words. Sheldon was then brought to the local wetlands for a burial at sea.

3:00 p.m.

Today, three neighbors had children graduating from another local high school. After the virtual graduation, they donned the caps and gowns and were out in front of their houses for pictures. The teachers hand-delivered the diplomas. They invited Natalie and another friend from the block to come down for pictures because they all grew up together.

Parents were all out in front. My friend Mike, who I have laughed with since childhood, was standing there with his wife Erin, so proud of their son who had just graduated. Still, I could see in their eyes, and every parent on the driveway, a little sting. It's that kick-in-the-gut emptiness that your child was deprived of something they worked hard to earn. Natalie says, "My friends and I are all going through it together, so it's not that bad."

I often forget that the teachable moments are not always parent or teacher to child. Some of the greatest come the other way.

As I walk back into the house, Joe says, "Dad, you know what I've been thinking?"

"No, what's that, buddy?"

"I've been thinking of how long it's been since we had a beef tenderloin."

With all they're going through, the least I can do is get a decent dinner. Went to Jack and Pat's, the go-to butcher on the south side. They have posted five warning signs as you walk in, not about the coronavirus.

"BEEF PRICES OUT OF CONTROL!"

I wasn't leaving. "How much is that seven-pound beef tenderloin?" I ask.

"$136.00 plus tax," he says, almost embarrassed.

I think again about all the kids have been going through.

"I'll take five stuffed pork chops."

They're kids, they'll be fine.

MAY 25: DAY 66

Landline call.

I answer, "Hello?"

"Mr. or Mrs. Heilmann, I'm calling from Best Vacations and we are prepared to offer you 90% on an all-inclusive vacation for you and your family: Tahoe, Mexico, Florida, oceanfront, the works. We know it's hard to travel but we'll give you two years. How does that sound?"

"I see. Do you know if any of these resorts have the virus?"

"All of these are five-star resorts, clean, best practices."

"Do they use Totally Awesome?"

"I'm sorry, sir, what?"

"Do these resorts use Totally Awesome cleaner? I don't stay at any resorts unless they use Totally Awesome cleaner."

Click.

It's Memorial Day.

The words of my neighbor Jordan, whose brother gave his life in service to the United States:

"Today and every day, my family and I are remembering, reflecting, and honoring the lives of all the service men and women who paid the ultimate sacrifice for our country. Especially my brother Jared Stanker and those of the 1-17 that didn't come home."

MAY 26: DAY 67

Researchers in Paris have now completed a one-month study, which revealed a new way to find out if there will be COVID outbreak in a city. They tested the raw sewage of residents for a month.

Disgusting. Who came up with that???? That's worse than remote learning.

The report says that "the technique can pick up a sharp rise in concentrations of the virus before there is an explosion in the clinic." An explosion. Nice choice of words.

"It's a cheap, non-invasive tool to warn of outbreaks." Oh, it's a little invasive.

11:30 a.m.

Brooke failed to read *Happy Birthday Mr. Kang*. We didn't get him a gift either.

"Brooke, why didn't you read *Happy Birthday Mr. Kang*?"

"Who is Mr. Kang?" she asks.

"I don't know. You have to read the story to find out. Now get down here."

"Can I do it later?"

"No, do it now."

"I don't wanna read it."

"YOU ARE GOING TO SIT DOWN AND READ *HAPPY BIRTHDAY MR. KANG*, DAMMIT!"

It's a real bad birthday for Mr. Kang.

Brooke also didn't finish her math, which means I need to help. I go to Pearson Realize and there are five little videos you have to watch. About halfway through the video, it stops and asks a question that you have to answer out loud. I finish the videos and hit *submit. Submit* is a good button for parents. This pops up:

> Are you sure you want to submit this when you haven't completed the work?

What work? There was no work. I had to answer a question out loud to an invisible class and I did. I said "three-fifths" out loud.

I repeat the process.

> Are you sure you want to turn the work in when it's not been completed?

It has. It has been completed. I email the teacher to tell her that Brooke didn't know what to do. The teacher wrote back, "It looks like you tried, so I'm going to give you full credit."

I know she pities me. I'll take a pity grade. I'm not above that.

MAY 27: DAY 68

10:30 a.m.

We are winding down. The books and computers get turned in this week. Every day I ask, "Are your assignments all turned in?" Every day my two angels look into their father's eyes and lie their little hearts out, "All done, Dad!"

The seventh-grade math teacher reaches out today. Mikey is missing four assignments. *Please get them in ASAP!*

He has to write expressions using the distributive, associative, and communist parties. Commutative properties. (Sorry, autocorrect).

Sabra joins a cooking club for $12.50 and pays $8.25 each month. She also joins a movie club for $14 and pays $8.75 each month. Write an expression for Sabra that tells her about the total amount of money she spends on both clubs after X months.

Well, here's an expression for you, Sabra. A penny saved is a penny earned. Recipes are free and Disney Plus is cheaper.

The third grade has to break words down by syllables.

Do you know the six syllable types? Closed, Open, Vowel-Silent E, Vowel Team, R-Controlled, and Consonant-L-E. Four useful syllable division patterns to follow are VC/CV, V/CV, VC/V, and V/V.

I will never, ne-ver forget the time I lost a job for not knowing this.

"Heilmann, get in here!"

"Yes, sir?"

"Now, before we sent out these invoices to the client, I asked you to break down every word by syllables—and this is what I get?"

"I'm sorry. I must have done the VC/CV instead of the VC/V."

"NOBODY FORGETS THAT AROUND HERE! You're GONE! Now GET OUT!"

While I tease, the breaking down of words by syllable helps children to read. The better they read, the more they will understand.

History Comes Alive Project

Today we have to finish this project on famous people in history. It has to be on that large three-panel foam board that's always on display at parent-teacher conferences. You walk by it and wonder why the one kid did such a terrible job and what's wrong with his parents.

Brooke is actually enjoying this project because the historic character she has chosen is William Shakespeare. Her mom taught Shakespeare.

It was fun getting her dressed in costume and watching Natalie fix her lice-free hair, draw on a mustache and beard, and of course, post it on TikTok.

One of the interesting facts about Shakespeare that Brooke discovered was that when he couldn't think of a word for something, he simply made one up.

Some words stand the test of time.

This above all. To thine own self be true.

MAY 28: DAY 69

I was told by a teacher today that twenty-four out of twenty-five kids in my son's class had the assignment turned in. Nice to be unique.

It's an exam on Romeo and Juliet.

IDENTIFY WHO IS SPEAKING:

And, if we meet, we shall not scape a brawl,

For now, these hot days, is the mad blood stirring.

It's either the Republicans or Democrats.

3:00 p.m.

HOMOPHONES AND HOMOGRAPHS

Whew. A lot of parents I spoke to were worried sick that we wouldn't get to these. You get the Constitution, fractions, and your homophones down and you have the basic building blocks for life.

Homographs, as you all know well, are words that are spelled the same but have different meanings. Do you know what example they gave?

BAT. A piece of sports equipment OR an animal.

Homophones. Words that sound alike but have different meanings.

There's the obvious one that jumps into your mind, galipot and gallipot, one being a type of turpentine exuded on the stem of certain types of species of a pine, and the other the well-known glazed pot used by apothecaries for medicine.

Hoard and horde.

> The horde of angry shoppers chose to hoard the toilet paper, leaving the nice dad without any.

One last one, cede and seed.

> It was during that time when parents had to cede their right to send children to school that they were most thankful the teachers had planted the right seed.

Tomorrow, May 29, they turn in their books.

MAY 29: DAY 70

This is a day we've been waiting for: May 29.

The governor has announced that the Phase 3 reopening begins today.

Gatherings up to ten people are allowed. Bars and restaurants can have outdoor seating, retail can open with capacity limits, and most importantly, the hair salons can open. Leona is happy.

Campgrounds are allowed to open, but with social distancing. I'm out. If I can't stay close to my fellow campers, forget it.

Also, employees of non-essential businesses can return to work. That's a nice category to be in, the non-essential, we can do without you, classification.

The Phase 3 is for the State of Illinois. Chicago is waiting until June 3.

More importantly, it's the last day of "real classes." School is not officially out until next week, but the students won't be doing anything. It's my obligation to contact the Cardinal and inform him of the mockery this principal is making of the Archdiocese.

One more lesson. Religion. They have to watch a video on forgiveness.

Why is it so hard to forgive? Forgiveness doesn't mean that you stop hurting from what someone has done to you. Doesn't mean you ever have to trust them. It only means that whatever a person owes you for the wrong, you're going to let that go. Why? Because it lets you move forward.

That's a good lesson.

MAY 30...

This chapter wasn't planned. Like so many in life.

May 29 was not supposed to end the way it did last night. Just when we thought we could get out and breathe a little, the air was sucked out of us. The video came out of a white Minneapolis police officer who put his knee on the neck of an African-American man for eight minutes during an arrest. That man, George Floyd, died. And the world was set on fire.

There were peaceful protests, and violent ones. There were prayers and there was stealing. There was screaming and there was silence. But the third largest city in the United States, on the verge of reopening, was shut down. It wasn't the protests we have seen in the past, where Lake Shore Drive or Michigan Avenue were shut down for a day. Thousands took to the streets as the entire country watched the literal and figurative fires burn.

What force could take a worldwide pandemic that had taken the lives of 450,000 people and knock it off the front page of the news? We had been living through "a first" in our lives. A health crisis with emergency orders to shelter–in-place, the closings of schools, churches, and businesses, and staying six feet away from everyone. Now, the very day we're supposed to get a little relief, we are hit with another first in our lives. A country that has been pushed over the edge.

Back-to-back firsts in the year 2020.

There is a lot of ugly out there. Maybe this is the stuff for Saint Drogos.

My children are watching this. But it's not 1967, when children might hear about this on the evening news. Their world is filled with millions of "virtual reporters" because technology has handed everyone the mic. The thoughts and opinions arrive unfiltered, non-stop. Too often with an annoying noise notification.

When they're confused, my kids ask for help. It's when they're not confused, when they think they have all the answers, that they *need* my help. I don't have all the answers. But hopefully a little wisdom comes with being in the high-risk category.

If I remember correctly from studying AP U.S. History with Natalie, there was this case back in 1967 called Loving v. Virginia. I also remember the movie. Mildred Jeter and Richard Loving were indicted by a Virginia Grand Jury for violating the state's ban on interracial marriages.

In June 1967, fifty-three years ago, a unanimous United States Supreme Court ruled in their favor.

This Court has consistently repudiated distinctions between citizens solely because of their ancestry as being odious to a free people whose institutions are founded upon the doctrine of equality. To deny this fundamental freedom on so unsupportable a basis as the racial classifications is directly subversive of the principle of equality at the heart of the Fourteenth Amendment. ..The Fourteenth Amendment requires that the freedom of choice to marry not be restricted by invidious racial discriminations. (1966) U.S. Reports: Loving v. Virginia, 388 U.S. 1

There will be a quiz on this at the end of the book.

While I didn't sit down and recite this Supreme Court holding to my children, we did talk. Like parents all over the country, I tried to find the right words.

I thought about my dad. He was a salesman. Worked two jobs so he could take care of my mom and six children, and never put himself ahead of giving to his family. He said that he had to be very careful about talking politics because he couldn't afford to lose customers and it was never worth losing a friend. Maybe staying quiet is one way of respecting the faith and politics of others, I don't know. I do know that when my parents saw us headed down the wrong path or making a dumb decision, they'd ask, "Do you think that's the right thing to do?" Simple, but effective.

I can't say what advice my children will hold onto from these seventy days. I do believe there are moments in history that kids remember what their parents told them while it was happening. I remember my father telling me to sit down and watch the Watergate hearings because it was history. This is one of those times.

Though the remote learning is over for now, we are still their first teachers.

A LETTER

Erica:

Well, sweetheart, that was the seventy days.

How I wish you were here to see it. It was like no other time in my life.

All we heard about for a while was "home." Shelter at home, school at home, stay at home, work at home, shop from home, calls to home about an extended car warranty.

I thought, how much can you learn in that environment? It all depends on what you choose to see.

Our kids saw being home as a sentence, while those in nursing homes would have found it a lifesaving gift. Millions were forced to work from home, while millions were at home out of work. While most took Zoom calls at home, doctors and nurses had a calling to leave their homes.

That they did, every day. While I was hyperventilating every time one of our children sneezed, these people left their homes and walked into hospitals knowing they could become infected, knowing they could bring a virus with no cure back to their own children. On the next vocabulary quiz, this is the new definition of selfless.

We heard the word *test* quite a bit. Tests in school, testing the e-learning system, testing work from home, and the testing of patients and patience. Like how I splashed in those homophones?

It was a test all right, one that was open-book, open-mind, open-heart and given to the entire planet. The subjects were science, medicine, history, faith, education, economics, finance, technology, health, and creative shopping. We couldn't cheat because no one had the answers.

Maybe we needed this test. If we understood the questions, then I think we'll pass and every generation after will be stronger for it.

The seventy days were stressful, confusing, sad, long, crazy, educational, and filled with so many raw emotions. But they were also funny. You have to see the humor in life's most anxious and stressful moments. We need it. In fact, the whole country could use a few more smiles right now.

I loved to make you laugh. I saw how it lifted, and if only for a few minutes, brought you away from the pain. I remember that office visit with our favorite oncologist, Dr. Pat, where you had been telling him for ten minutes straight about the pain, nausea, hand tremors, and lousy side effects of the chemo you were on, and he looked up and said, "Why does this have to be all about you? What about my feelings?"

You laughed so hard. He knew his audience and how to lift. And it did.

I hope that during this pandemic—whether it was a funny text, viral video, great impersonation, creative TikTok, what we saw at the grocery store, or a hysterical story—that those of us still here learned the value of humor in the "serious" parts of our lives. That's when humor has its greatest impact. And it is infectious.

If there is something else out there that can improve health, lower stress, relieve pain, stimulate creativity, boost collaboration, disarm, connect, build trust, promote social bonds, lift emotionally, bring people together and be the best means of communication in today's world, I can't think of it.

You loved to laugh. What I would give to make you smile one more time. You also gave the best hugs. The virus took away a lot of hugs. I missed them and learned the next time to hold on a little tighter. There was so much to learn. There was so much to see.

The pain of death, the joy of health, the power of a touch.

The courage of those who risk their health and lives to save ours.

The intelligence and drive of those who seek cures.

All that teachers give to our children to help them learn. Every single day.

The incredible benefit of having a thoughtful employer.

The unfairness and inequities of disease.

The importance of saving when times are good, because we never know what can happen.

The cruelty of a murder hornet.

The need for humor.

The depth of patience.

How our children can teach us, if we're willing to listen.

How precious that time is before your child goes to college.

The good fortune of technology.

Never to hurt the only lungs we have.

How children learn responsibility and deadlines.

How a virus can spread.

How long six feet is.

A small thing like washing your hands.

Our own strength and resilience.

How hard it is to find a vaccine, even when the smartest people in the world are trying.

How precious life is and how quickly it can be taken away.

The warmth of being close.

How far we have come in one hundred years.

That need for comfort and support from as many of our family and friends as we can get, when we lose someone.

If you give more understanding than you have received, you'll likely get more than you can give.

That toilet paper can run out.

Time. Maybe the most important lesson of all.

Time was given to us. Everything was canceled. Families were told to stay home. Together. It may have been one of the greatest gifts of time.

I saw four children who may never spend this much time together again in their lives. And I knew it was precious time I had with them.

As we were being given more time, others were losing it fast. Everyone who was sick, or who had a loved one in the hospital or a nursing home, needed more. To find a cure, to recover, to hold the hand of someone they loved and say those words that need to be said.

When we are about to take our last breath, the one thing that we most want is time. We have love. We need time.

Erica, you and I know this too well.

This year, when the world stopped, I hope we had a better chance to see. It is 2020 after all. It may have been the greatest learning period of our lives.

That's what happened during the seventy days, sweetheart. I'll tell you more about it when I see you.

Love you most.

And that's it. That's it.

BEFORE YOU GO

Thanks so much for allowing me to spend time with you as you read this book. I'd like to take just a few more minutes to make a small request.

If you enjoyed this book, gained even just a few insights that were helpful to you, please share them with others. I also invite you to share what you have learned with those inside and outside your family who you believe could benefit from this book.

But most of all, please share what you felt were relevant and interesting on Amazon with a paragraph or two review. Amazon is where more than two-thirds of all books are sold. I would sincerely welcome your personal thoughts.

How to Leave a Review?

Just go to Amazon (www.amazon.com), look up the title, and then type in a short review. Even if you only have read a couple of chapters, leaving reviews make all the difference to the success of a book. Your impressions and takeaways matter.

In our content-cluttered world, books succeed by the kind, generous time readers take to leave honest reviews. I thank you in advance for this very kind gesture. And, finally, if you would like to reach out to me with questions or comments about the book, please feel free to email me at daveheilmann1@gmail.com.

ACKNOWLEDGEMENTS

My love and thanks to Natalie, Joey, Mikey and Brooke. Too many days I have sat at the computer and not given you the time you deserve from your father. You will never know all that you give your dad every day, including some wonderful stories.

Thanks to my Mom Therese, sisters Cathy, Diane, and Suzy, brother John, and the Joes in heaven, my dad and brother. You are the seven people who most influenced the importance of humor and laughter in my life.

Thank you to my mother-in-law Leona, because without your constant help and bringing a little part of Erica to us every day, this book wouldn't have been written.

Glen and Gary, as we share the hard days, I am thankful that you are always there to help us find better ones.

A very special thank you to Teri Goudie. You are the strategic communications coach to the world, but more importantly, my friend. By saying to me during the hardest moments of my life, "let's bring the value of humor to leaders and organizations everywhere," you pulled me up at the time I needed it most.

Thank you, Caylen Bufalino and Jim Hutchinson, who along with Teri are my partners known as the Headliners Consultants. As we look to provide uniquely entertaining communication training through the power of humor, music, and education, you opened my mind to writing this little book during the virus.

Special thanks to Tara Lewis, who edited this book, not only for her talents but her kindness and invaluable feedback throughout the writing process.

Thank you to Melissa G Wilson founder of Networlding Publishing and book-creation coach. When I first started telling Melissa about this story, she immediately embraced the project and has been supportive and my guide every step of the way.

Thank you to my partners at Clausen Miller, top tier litigators who also know the importance of relationships and a smile.

Finally, thanks to my sweetheart Erica, who in too few years gave me inspiration and love for a lifetime.